# ERICH FROMM

# Love, Sexuality, and Matriarchy

## About Gender

Edited and with an introduction by
### Dr. Rainer Funk

FROMM INTERNATIONAL PUBLISHING CORPORATION
NEW YORK

FIRST FROMM INTERNATIONAL EDITION, 1997

Copyright © 1997 Fromm International
Copyright © 1994 German-language edition DTV GmbH
For copyrights of individual contributions see page 219

All rights reserved under International Pan-American copyright
convention. Published in the United States by Fromm International
Publishing Corporation, New York. First published by DTV
GmbH & Co. KG, Munich under the title *Liebe, Sexualität und
Matriarchat.*

LIBRARY OF CONGRESS CATALOGING-IN-PUBLICATION DATA

Fromm, Erich, 1900–
    [Liebe, Sexualität und matriarchat. English]
    Love, sexuality, and matriarchy : about gender / Erich Fromm ;
edited and with an introduction by Rainer Funk. — 1st Fromm
International ed.
        p.  cm.
    Includes bibliographical references and index.
    ISBN 0-88064-186-X
    1. Sex role.  2. Sex differences (Psychology)  3. Matriarchy.
4. Patriarchy.  5. Sex (Psychology)  6. Love.    I. Funk, Rainer.
II. Title.
    HQ1075.F7513  1997
    306.7—dc21                                        97-38333
                                                          CIP

10  9  8  7  6  5  4  3  2  1

Manufactured in the United States of America

# Contents

# CONTENTS

Social Character and Love

# Editor's Introduction

We will never understand the psychology of either women or men as long as we fail to acknowledge that a state of war has existed between the sexes for approximately six thousand years. This war is a guerrilla war. Six thousand years ago the patriarchy triumphed over women, and society became organized on the basis of male domination. Women became the property of men and were obliged to be grateful to them for every concession. But there cannot be domination of one social class, nation, or sex over the other that does not lead to subliminal rebelliousness, rage, hatred, and desire for revenge in those who are oppressed and exploited, and to fear and insecurity in those who do the oppressing and exploiting." This statement was made by Erich Fromm in an interview appearing in the February 16, 1975, issue of the Italian magazine *L'Espresso*. It sums up his basic thinking concerning the problematic relations between men and women. It is not the difference between them that inevitably leads to difficulties for both sexes but the use that is made of this difference.

Fromm is not primarily interested in the existence of anatomical and biological differences between the sexes but in how these differences have been made use of throughout human history. The difference between the sexes—the otherness of the opposite sex—in combination with sexuality has the function of assuring human survival. The attraction of one sex for the other apparently has a very limited significance in keeping human beings from using sexual difference for the purpose of domination. What *is* of primary interest concerning the problem between the sexes is the psychological effect the functioning of this difference has on an individual's sense of identity and on human relationships, especially between persons of opposite sexes.

Any solution to the problem that merely attempts to transfer domination from men to women only fosters the warfare between them. For this reason, in the 1975 interview mentioned above, Fromm does not favor a movement for women's rights that in reality "retains the principles of the patriarchal world, except that women now will have the power that was formerly the exclusive domain of men," for this would mean that women are not "being emancipated as human beings." The war would then continue and "inevitably produce a great deal of hatred and sadism on both sides. The exploited and the exploiters are sitting in the same boat, like prisoners and their wardens. Each group threatens the other and hates the other. Each fears the attacks of the other. Even though men pretend otherwise, they nonetheless do fear women."

There is scarcely any psychological issue that arouses so much controversy and is so complex as that of relations between the sexes. The reason is simple: because we still find ourselves in the patriarchal tradition, everyone is affected by this issue and is also biased, participating in transferences and projections that are common in "the war of the sexes." If we are to find a path to clarity here we must become aware of our own involvement in the patriarchal mind-set as we develop some sense of what matriarchal patterns of perception and thought really are. Only in this way can we glimpse and subsequently adopt a view of reality that reconciles the difference between the sexes.

Any meaningful investigation of the problem of the relationship between men and women must begin with the use that has been made of the difference between them since the establishment of the patriarchy. Fromm himself came to this realization as early as the end of the 1920s after reading the works of Johann Jakob Bachofen and as a result of conversations with the Baden-Baden physician Georg Groddeck. It is impossible to overestimate the importance Bachofen's work *Mother Right* had for the development of Fromm's thought. A first testament to Bachofen's influence is found in Fromm's writings in the early 1930s, and his high regard for Bachofen can be traced throughout his entire work. In his old age Fromm still counted Bachofen among the most important sources of his thought, and he never tired of recommending *Mother Right* to others.

The essays in the first part of this collection bear eloquent testimony to Fromm's favorable reaction to Bachofen's ideas concerning matriarchal and patriarchal social structures. He not only demonstrates his enthusiasm for Bachofen's views but also shows himself to be a prophetic thinker who recognized the central importance of the problems inherent in relations between men and women, which have become such a burning issue today. I should like to comment on two essays from Part I that are published here for the first time:

"Bachofen's Discovery of the Mother Right" was found posthumously in manuscript form in English among Fromm's professional papers. It was written in the mid-1950s as an introduction to a projected English translation of Bachofen's *Mother Right* that apparently didn't materialize at the time. It was not until 1967 that the Bollingen Foundation sponsored the translation of Bachofen's main works. Fromm's introduction, originally entitled "Bachofen's Significance for Today," was subsequently forgotten and never published by its author.

It was only recently that I discovered the essay "The Male Creation" in the portion of Fromm's papers to be found in the New York Public Library. It was handwritten in German. The date of 1933 assigned to it is not certain. The manuscript's explicit mention of *American* as well as European culture leads one to suspect that the piece was written in the first months after Fromm's emigration to the United States. In his later works he returns again and again to the comparison presented in this essay between the biblical and the Babylonian creation myths.

Matriarchal and patriarchal social structures determine relations between the sexes in essential ways. Yet they are not the only determining factors. In the second part of the present volume Fromm investigates whether there is a connection between sex and character; his essay of 1943 on this subject attempts to demonstrate that biological differences between men and women lead to certain characterological ones. His discussion focuses on the differing roles of male and female in sexual intercourse and the resulting characterological differences. These differences of course are intertwined with those produced directly by social factors, which are "much stronger in their effect and can either increase, eliminate, or reverse biologically rooted differences." In 1948 Fromm added important passages to this essay, which are included for the first time in the version presented here.

Fromm's second contribution to the subject of sexual differences and character bears the title "Man–Woman," in its original form a lecture he delivered in 1949. Published in 1951, it represents a theoretical departure from the essay "Sex and Character" in that Fromm no longer attempts to deduce characterological differences between men and women from biological factors but states in lapidary fashion that it is not true that "the difficulties in the relationship between man and woman are essentially due to the difference in sex." What matters first and foremost is that it is a relationship between human beings. And this relationship is defined by the dominant "social character" at the time. The dominant social character of *our* time is distinguished by the fact that people no longer look to their intrinsic individuality and their sex-specific essence for fulfillment but are governed by the market, by success, by the expectations of others, by the role assigned them. The market demands that "our male or female roles become obscured." There is very little of a sex-specific nature left in the relationship between men and women.

Fromm believes the difference between the sexes is shaped by matriarchal and patriarchal social structures as well as by the dominant orientation of the social character at a given time. This has far-reaching consequences for the role of, as well as our view of, sexuality in the context of sexual differences. The third section of this book treats the connection between gender and sexuality in two essays. The first, "Sex and Character," was written in 1948 in response to the publication of the Kinsey Report, although Fromm deals with that report only peripherally. Contrary to Freud, who traces the character of a man or woman back to the direction the sex drive took in childhood, Fromm explains the connection in exactly opposite terms: "In my view, sexual behavior is not the cause but the effect of a person's character structure." It is not "the bed" that determines the success or failure of a relationship but the nature of the relationship, the characterological orientation, that determines sexual behavior. Sex-specific problems thus do not result from the difference between the sexes but are primarily the expression of the particular manner in which two people relate to each other.

This applies not only to the forms of heterosexuality but to those of homosexuality as well. Fromm made just a few passing remarks on the subject of homosexuality. The essay "Changing Concepts of Homosexuality" is his only separate work on the topic. Found among his papers located in New York, it was written in English around 1940. In it Fromm points out that Freud's concept of homosexuality is not verified in therapeutic practice. According to Fromm, homosexuality is not a separate clinical entity but a symptom that can accompany the most diverse characterological problems and that "tends to disappear when the general character problems are solved." This, Fromm believes, confirms his view that it is not sexuality which shapes character but characterological orientation which shapes sexual behavior. Accordingly, there are "as many variations of homosexual behavior as of heterosexual, and the interpersonal relations of homosexuals show the same problems as those of heterosexuals."

The problems in relationships between men and women that accompany sexual differences are not primarily a result of the latter; rather, these differences are used as a means to gratify passions (character traits) such as domination and submission, love and hatred. Therefore, the most important question concerning relations between the sexes is which characterological orientation determines human relationships: love or hate, love of life or fascination with force. The fourth section of this book deals with these basic orientations.

The article "Selfishness and Self-Love" appeared in the journal *Psychiatry* in 1939, and except for its first part, which Fromm included in his book *Man for Himself* (1947), it received no notice. Yet it is among his most important essays. Here he develops—long before the exponents of a psychology of the self and the theory of narcissism—a theory of the self in which, unlike Freud, he maintains that one's relatedness to oneself always corresponds to one's relatedness to others. Instead of assuming competition between self-love and love of others, Fromm posits a correspondence and correlation between relatedness to self and relatedness to objects, emphasizing the need for a positive relatedness to oneself, namely self-love. Only when this need has been thwarted do selfishness and narcissism arise as forms of compensation for the lack of self-love. He finds that the same logic connecting love of self and love of others applies to hate, and he speaks of both a reactive and a character-conditioned hate. Surprising here is the clarity with which Fromm in 1939 shed light on the psychological roots of National Socialism in Germany. (Dividing Fromm's essay into sections with headings is my addition.)

Love and hate are basic character orientations; they shape relations between the sexes. In the course of the twentieth century love and hate have taken on a much more comprehensive and also a more precise significance: Not simply love but love for life itself, for what grows and develops—biophilia. Hate too has reached beyond itself; it has become the desire for destruction for its own sake, attraction to all that is lifeless, fascination with violence, love for what is dead: necrophilia. This is the subject of the last essay in this volume, which appeared in an American periodical in 1967. It will not be the gender conflict which will determine humanity's future but whether we opt for love of life or love of death. This is what will rule our relationships, including those between the sexes. Love of life, however, is "difficult to experience in a culture that emphasizes results instead of processes, things instead of life, that makes means into ends and teaches us to use the brain when the heart should be involved. Love for another person and love for life are not something that can be achieved in a hurry. Sex, yes, but not love. Love requires pleasure in stillness, an ability to enjoy *being* instead of *doing, having,* or *using.*"

Rainer Funk
—*Translated by Hunter Hannum
and Hildegarde Hannum*

# I

## Mother Right and Male Creation

# 1

## Bachofen's Discovery of the Mother Right (1955)

Bachofen is known only to relatively few specialists. Yet he is by no means a "forgotten author"; he was never well known or famous, not even at the time of the publication of his books, or shortly after his death. In the last years of his life, his work found admiring recognition by some anthropologists, such as Adolf Bastian and Lewis H. Morgan, and by Friedrich Engels who (together with Karl Marx) was greatly impressed by Bachofen's work. Many years passed in which Bachofen was almost completely ignored, until in the years before the first World War a small group of romantically minded German intellectuals started to read Bachofen again, and to spread his name, although only in small circles. It is only in recent years that a new growing interest in Bachofen can be observed, not only in Germany and Switzerland, but also in English- and Spanish-speaking countries.

The peculiar fate of Bachofen's work becomes even more highlighted if we compare him with another genius working a generation later on closely related problems, Sigmund Freud.

What contrast in the fate of their work! Freud becomes one of the best-known thinkers of the world, his ideas and terms household words for everybody, his books published in all languages, his ideas taught at numerous institutes; on the other hand, Bachofen, a figure unknown to the great public, admired by a few, and ridiculed by most specialists. This is all the more striking if one considers that Bachofen sometimes anticipated Freud's ideas, sometimes gave more profound answers to the same questions.

Bachofen's central discovery is usually considered to be that of the Mother Right. On the basis of his analysis of Roman, Greek, and Egyptian myths and symbols, he came to the conclusion that the patriarchal structure of society as we know it throughout the history of the civilized world is of a relatively recent date, and that it was preceded by a state of culture in which the mother was the head of the family, the ruler in society, and the Great Goddess. He assumed, furthermore, that the matriarchal phase was preceded, in the very beginning of history, by a cruder, less civilized form of society ("hetaerism"), based entirely on the natural productiveness of the woman, without marriage, law, principles, or order, a state of life to be compared with the wild growth of swamp plants. The matriarchal phase is in the middle between that lowest, and the highest phase of human development so far, that of patriarchy, in which the father rules, as the representative of the principle of law, reason, conscience, and hierarchical social organization.

This theory is more than an anthropological hypothesis concerning certain prehistorical phenomena. It is a sweeping and profound philosophy of history, in many ways similar to those of Hegel and particularly Marx. For Marx, history begins with an original state of equality but at the same time with little self-awareness, and yet small productive forces. Man develops through the evolution of labor, he develops his reason, his

4

skill, his individuality; eventually he returns to the original harmony, but on a new level of rationality and technique. For Bachofen, a similar course of evolution is centered around the dominant role of the mother and the father figures respectively. History moves from the prerational motherly world through the rational patriarchal world, but at the same time from freedom and equality to hierarchy and inequality. Eventually man will return to the establishment of love and equality on a new level, a hypothesis of matriarchal-patriarchal principles.

The significance of Bachofen is by no means exhausted by this evolutionary scheme of history. By his analysis of the nature of motherly and fatherly love, Bachofen has paved a way into the very center of psychology, of individual and social psychic development; he is not a "forerunner" of modern psychology, but rather a pathfinder who has given us insights which now, after a hundred years of development of the science of man, are more fruitful or, paradoxically, more up-to-date than even in his own time. The following remarks are meant to give same substance to this statement.

The most fundamental achievement of Bachofen is, perhaps, his analysis of the essence of motherly and fatherly love and, correspondingly, of the difference between the attachment to mother and to father respectively. He is not concerned with the empirical mother and father of this or that person, but with the "ideal type" of mother and of father (in Max Weber's sense), or the motherly and fatherly archetypes (in Jung's sense). He examines the function and role of the motherly and the fatherly principle in human evolution.

What is the nature of the motherly function?

"Raising her young, the woman learns earlier than the man to extend her loving care beyond the limits of the ego to another creature, and to direct whatever gift of invention she possesses to the preservation and improvement of this other's existence. Woman at this stage is the repository of all culture, of a benevolence, of all devotion, of all concern for the living and grief for the dead." (Bachofen 1967, 79)

Love, care, responsibility for others, are the creations of the mother; motherly love is the seed from which all love and altruism grows. But beyond that, motherly love is the basis for the development of universal humanism. The mother loves her children because they are her children, not because they fulfill this or that condition or expectation. Mother loves her children equally, hence her children experience themselves as equals inasmuch as their central attachment is that to mother. "The idea of motherhood produces a sense of universal fraternity among all men, which dies with the development of paternity." (*Ibid.*, 80) As a further consequence, the basic principles of the mother-centered culture are those of freedom and equality, of happiness and the unconditional affirmation of life.

In contrast to the motherly principles the fatherly principle is that of law, order, reason, hierarchy; the father has his favorite son, the one who is most like him, the most suited to become the heir and successor to his property and worldly functions. Among the father-centered sons, equality has given way to hierarchy, harmony to strife. It is the greatness of Bachofen to have shown the progress in evolution from the matriarchal to the patriarchal principle in history, and yet to have recognized both the positive and the negative aspects of the matriarchal and the patriarchal principles, respectively. Considering the patriarchate the higher form of evolution does not lead him to ignore the specific virtues of the matriarchal structure, nor does he fail to see the vices of patriarchism.

The positive aspect of matriarchism lies in the sense of equality, universality, and unconditional affirmation of life. The negative aspect lies in its bondage to blood and soil, its lack of rationality and progress. The positive aspect of patriarchism lies in its principle of reason, law, science, civilization, spiritual development; its negative aspect in hierarchy, oppression, inequality, inhumanity. The positive aspects of matriarchism and the negative aspects of patriarchism are nowhere more clearly represented than in Aeschylus' Antigone. Antigone is the representative of humanity and love; Creon, the totalitarian leader, the representative of state worship and obedience.

Beyond his discovery of the essence of motherly and fatherly love and the role of both principles in history, Bachofen is truly the father of the interpretation of symbols and myths, as Freud was the father of dream interpretation. To be sure, Bachofen's interest in the myth was part of an interest he shared with romantics such as Karl Otfried Mueller, Joseph von Goerres or Georg Friedrich Creuzer. But Bachofen is of a truly genial originality in his method of uncovering the unconscious behind the latent content of the myth. With painstaking attention to the detail of the myth, Bachofen succeeds in following through from this surface to the deepest unconscious roots and motivations of the myth.

He had a gift of intuiting and then proving the meaning of symbols rarely to be found in other scholars. Anyone who wants to learn the understanding of the richness and subtlety of symbolism can hardly find a better teacher than Bachofen in his myth interpretations. In reading, for instance, the chapter on the Egg-symbols one will not only understand the depth and subtlety necessary for the interpretation of the symbol, but also the extraordinary patience and love for his subject which characterizes every one of Bachofen's steps in unraveling the meaning of a symbol or a myth. Bachofen himself was quite aware of the richness and depth of the myth which permits not only of one "correct" interpretation, but of several, according to the depth of understanding one has arrived at. The myth, the exegesis of the symbol, is the "product of a cultural period in which life had not yet broken away from the harmony of nature . . ." (*Ibid.*, 76) The myth has its own laws, and once one knows these laws its understanding has the same objective and rational validity as that of any other historical phenomenon.

This leads us to consider Bachofen's method and approach to the interpretation of myths and symbols. First, and perhaps most important, Bachofen is not impressed by existing opinions. He is clearly aware of the opposition his theories will provoke.

"This contrast, which indeed could scarcely be more radical, exerts a profound effect both on our methods and on our findings. The findings carry us back to historical facts which a dogmatic prejudice regards as no longer valid, and which are nevertheless essential to any general understanding of history." (*Ibid.*, 241–42)

Such an approach depends largely on one condition.

"The scholar must be able to renounce entirely the ideas of his own time, the beliefs with which these have filled his spirit, and transfer himself to the midpoint of a completely different world of thought. Without such self-abnegation no real success in the study of antiquity is thinkable. The scholar who takes the attitude of later generations as his starting point will inevitably be turned away from an understanding of the earliest time. The contradictions multiply; when it seems impossible to explain a phenomenon, the only way out seems to be to doubt and ultimately deny its existence. And that is why the scholarship and criticism of our time produces so few great and lasting results. True criticism resides in the material itself, and knows no other standard than its own objective law; no other aim than to understand the alien system; no other test than the number of phenomena which its basic principle explains. Where scholarship requires distortions, the falsification rests with the scholar and not with the sources to which, in his ignorance, arrogance, and carelessness, he likes to impute his own failings. The serious scholar must bear in mind that the world he is exploring is infinitely different from the one he is familiar with, and that his knowledge of it, however considerable, must always be limited; that his experience of life is usually immature, based as it is on the observation of a brief interval of time, while the material at his disposal is a heap of isolated ruins and fragments which often, seen from a single angle, seem inauthentic, but later, when transposed into their true context, belie such premature judgment." (*Ibid.*, 81–82)

In this passage Bachofen has not only given one of the most succinct and beautiful expressions of the problem of objectivity and inner freedom in historical research, he has also given a true picture of his own approach. By reading his work one is struck—and the more so the further one proceeds—by the objectivity of Bachofen. He is not impressed—as little as his great compatriot Carl Jacob Burckhardt—by the noise of contemporary power and success, and not even his own predilections and values make him distort the picture of the past. Bachofen called his method "eine naturforschende Methode" (*Ibid.*, 242), by which he means a "purely objective observation," (*Ibid.*) and one must read his account of the various aspects of this method to get a full impression of the unique qualities of Bachofen as an observer and scientist.

*Mutterrecht* was published at around the same time as Darwin's chef d'oeuvre. And in spite of the many obvious differences between Darwin's and Bachofen's works there is no mistaking the fact that Bachofen applied the evolutionary principle to the development of man and history. He, too, sees the beginning of human evolution as lowly, and even humiliating to our pride.

"Even though the picture that unrolls before us may offer little comfort, even though it may not encourage much pride in our beginnings, still, the spectacle of man gradually transcending the bestial in his nature may offer firm ground for a confident belief that through all vicissitudes the human race will find the power to complete its triumphant journey upward from the depths, from the night of matter to the light of a celestial-spiritual principle." (*Ibid.*, 185)

And:

"Who would not like to . . . spare our race the memory of so unworthy a childhood? But the testimony of history forbids us to heed the voices of pride and self-love. It cannot be doubted that the institution of marriage was the outgrowth of a very slow progress." (*Ibid.*, 93)

We cannot leave this short description of Bachofen's method without at least mentioning briefly his dialectic approach. As for Hegel, conflict and contradiction for Bachofen is the midwife of progress. Each historical phenomenon is to be understood as a reaction to an earlier and opposite state. "It is no paradox but a great truth . . . that human culture advances only through the clash of opposites." (*Ibid.*, 227) Equipped with this understanding of the dialectic nature of the historical process, Bachofen could see that the very extreme of an attitude results from its having overcome a preceding opposite state, and that if one digs only deep enough, one still finds in the new extreme remains of the preceding opposite. (Cf. Freud's "return of the repressed" in the concept of reaction formation.)

No wonder that a man with a truly scientific spirit, like Bachofen, was not impressed by the quantitative method in the social sciences. The thorough and exhausting analysis of one phenomenon is more valuable than the demonstration of many parallels, none of which is quite convincing. For Bachofen a hundred half-proofs never added up to the proof given by one thorough analysis. He showed that one cannot separate the understanding of social structure, law, religion, family constellation, and character structure from one another. An insight which has been gaining ground only in the last years, was fully grasped and applied by Bachofen a hundred years ago. Thus, by virtue of this very insight, Bachofen is neither an anthropologist, an archaeologist, a philosopher, a psychologist, a sociologist, a historian. He is a student of the science of man, for whom none of these aspects exists independently from one another.

I pointed to the peculiar contradiction between the fate of Bachofen's and of Freud's work. Indeed, there are other important differences in the work and personalities of these two men—but they also serve to emphasize the striking similarities.

Their work is centered around the same problem, that of understanding the development of man by understanding the development of his relationship to mother and father. Both for Bachofen and for Freud, human development begins with the attachment to mothers which then is dissolved and replaced by the relationship to father as the central figure of affection. But what a difference in the meaning of this attachment! For Freud it was primarily a sexual attachment; by this very assumption, Freud obscured the fact which Bachofen had brought to light, that the relationship to mother is the first and the most intense emotional relationship of the little child. The strongest longing in the infant, a longing which never leaves man until, indeed, he returns to mother earth, is the longing for mother's love; mother for him is life, warmth, food, happiness, security. It is unconditional love, the experience of being loved not because I am obedient, good, useful—but because I am mother's child, because I am in need of love and protection. Freud, probably due to reasons rooted in his own character, rationalized, as it were, this strongest of all affective yearnings into a sexual attachment, based on the fact that the little boy has an already active sexual instinct and that mother

11

is the only woman he knows intimately, and who in the process of caring for him physically even stimulates his sexual desires. Freud showed his strange denial of the emotional significance of mother by saying "I could not point to any need in childhood as strong as that for a father's protection." (Freud 1953, 21) Or, after his father's death, in the Introduction to the second edition of his *Interpretation of Dreams*, 1908: that a father's death is "the most important event, the most poignant loss, in a man's life" (Jones 1953, Vol. I, 324) One can clearly see how in Freud's own experience mother has been eliminated from her central role, and dethroned for the sake of the father. The Goddess is driven out, and transformed into the prostitute.

Bachofen, with his interpretation, teaches how right Freud was when he assumed that inability to overcome the fixation to mother (although not all the longing for her) is the nucleus of all neurosis—and he demonstrates how wrong Freud was in narrowing down the role of mother to that of a sexual one. It is Bachofen's fundamental discovery that the earliest and most profound attachment of man is that to mother, that the development into maturity, both as far as the race and the individual is concerned, depends on man's ability to overcome this fixation and to go through the stage of making the relationship to father the central one; eventually, that on a still higher level of development, the bond to mother is renewed, but not any more as a fixation to one's individual mother, but as a return to the principles of love and equality on a higher spiritual level.

While Freud, from his extreme patriarchal standpoint, saw woman as a castrated man (a typical compensation for the unresolved fear of a dependence on women), Bachofen saw in her, as mother, the representative of a primal force, of nature, reality, and at the same time of love and affirmation of life. Because of this, and not because of her sexual appeal, exists an attachment which is so difficult to overcome. On the other hand, showing the positive function of the father, Bachofen makes it clear that the turn from mother to father is not due to the castration threat, but to the boy's need for guidance and help by the fatherly principle embodied by the father.

Bachofen delved into the mystery of symbolic language, as Freud did. Freud studied mainly the dream—Bachofen the myth. They both were unimpressed by the conventional opinions about myths and dream; they both were looking for the hidden, latent, unconscious meaning of dreams and myths. But here again, what difference in the depth of expression of the most elementary strivings of man, rooted in the very conditions of his existence; Freud restricting the meaning much too often to sexuality or to connections—and often trivial ones, brought about by free association.

Again, both Bachofen and Freud are concerned with the relationship among history, religion, and psychology. Bachofen sees the evolution of the human race as one of emergence from the tie to mother and makes a construction of matriarchal society as preceding the patriarchal cultures known to us. Freud, on the contrary, lets history and human evolution begin with the father-dominated herd and the rebellion of the sons against the father.

The theoretical similarities and differences between Bachofen and Freud only mirror the similarities and differences of their personalities. Both were men of genius with an unquenchable passion for the truth, an insatiable interest in the hidden, mysterious underworld of the spirit. Yet, what differences. Bachofen, the Swiss patrician—religious, conservative, and antiliberal. Freud, the Viennese Jew—liberal, antireligious, rationalistic.

Yet these differences cover up others which are not less significant. Bachofen, though extremely conservative and deeply suspicious of modern progress, was a man of profound faith

13

in the future of the human race. He believed that the beginning and the end of human affairs show a peculiar similarity, and that the end is the return to the beginning, on a higher level of development. The principles of matriarchy are not simply to disappear, but will be conserved ("aufgehoben" in Hegel's sense) and united with the principles of patriarchy in a new synthesis. These are Bachofen's own words in which he describes his faith in the development of the human race:

"One great law governs the juridical development of man. It advances from the material to the immaterial, from the physical to the metaphysical, from tellurism to spirituality. The ultimate goal can be attained only through the united effort of all peoples and ages, but attained it assuredly will be despite all ups and downs. What begins materially must end immaterially. At the end of all juridical development there stands a new *ius naturale*, now not of matter but of spirit; an ultimate justice which will be universal, just as the primordial justice was universal; which, like the primordial law, will be free from all arbitrariness; dictated by the things themselves; not invented but discovered by man, just as the primordial physical law appeared as an immanent material order. The Persians believed that there would someday be one justice and one language. *When Ahriman is destroyed the earth will be flat and level, and happy mankind will have one mode of life, one form of government, and one language.* (Plutarch, *De Isis et Osiris* 47.) This last justice expresses the pure radiance of the good principle. It is not tellurian like the bloody dark justice of the first material era, but celestial and luminous, the perfect law of Zeus. But its ultimate sublimation must also imply its dissolution. Through liberation from all material admixture, law becomes love. Love is the highest justice. And this justice again appears in the dual, but not, like the old tellurian justice, in the duality of conflict and never-ending annihilation—now it discloses the duality that offers the other cheek and gladly gives away the second cloak. In this doctrine the highest justice is realized. Its perfection transcends even the concept of justice and so becomes the ultimate and complete negation of matter, the resolution of all dissonance." (Bachofen 1967, 189–90)

In spite of, or perhaps because of, this faith in man, Bachofen was utterly skeptical about the "progress" of his time, and about what was to come in the twentieth century. Here is a prediction regarding the future of the world, written in 1869, which shows the prophetic clarity with which Bachofen could see the future, the same intuitive clarity with which he saw the past:

"I begin to believe that for the historians of the twentieth century there will be nothing to write about but America and Russia. The old world of Europe lies ailing and will never recover for good. Then our use to the new rulers of the world will be as teachers, just as the Greeks had been to Rome's leaders, and we will have the opportunity to study thoroughly the history of this progress near its end. Unfortunately, I am a pessimist, the unpopular kind." (to Meyer-Ochsner on May 25, 1969.)

Freud's political attitude is the opposite in a paradoxical manner. He, the liberal, has little faith in the future of mankind. Even if the social and economic problems could be solved, he believes, man's nature would still make him jealous and envious of other men, he would still be driven by the wish to compete with other men for the prerogative of possessing all desirable women. For Freud, the historical process is essentially tragic. The more man creates cultures the more does he frustrate his instinctual drives, the more unhappy and neurotic does he become. For Bachofen, man develops through conflicts to ever higher forms of harmony. On the other hand, Bachofen was never impressed by power, while

Freud was. As Jones, in the second volume of his biography of Freud describes, Freud became an ardent patriot when the first World War started, deeply convinced of the righteousness of Austria's and Germany's cause, excited and enthusiastic about the German victories. This tragic fall into war hysteria could not have happened to Bachofen; for him, spiritual realities and values were too real and definite to ever lead him into the worship of arms and victories.

This comparison between Bachofen and Freud is not meant to detract from Freud's greatness; greatness remains even though shadows mar the brightness of a genius's figure. The comparison was made in order to clarify the specific position of Bachofen and perhaps to give expression to my personal admiration for a man who is so little known and yet has so much to give to our generation and to the future.

This leads me to some concluding remarks about the problem, in which directions can Bachofen's work be continued and used as a source for new discoveries in anthropology, history, religion, and psychology. In one field Bachofen has already had considerable influence in the past; in that of the studies of Marx and Engels concerned with the connection among family structure, the structure of society, and economic organization in early history. Engels, in his book on *The Origin of the Family, Private Property, and the State* (first published in 1884) gives testimony to the impact of Bachofen's thought on his own. Others, like Lewis H. Morgan in his *Systems of Consanguinity and Affinity of the Human Family* (1871) and in *Ancient Society* (1887), and many years later Robert Briffault in his book *The Mothers* brought forth evidence for the existence of the matriarchal structure in many societies and religions other than the ones studied by Bachofen. But this constitutes only a beginning in making Bachofen's discoveries fertile for the study of anthropology and history. The study of Hinduism, Mexican and Chinese religions, of the development of Judaism, Catholicism, and Protestantism, will result in new and revealing insights when Bachofen's basic ideas are applied. His theories will also throw a great deal of light on primitive religions and on pseudoreligious phenomena like the modern totalitarian system. A full understanding of their effect and attraction on millions of people will be possible only by seeing how the motherly and the fatherly functions are blended, and appeal to the unconscious longings in both directions.

Not less fruitful will be the application of Bachofen's theories to the field of individual psychology. It will lead to the necessary correction of Freud's concept of incest and the Oedipus complex, and to the deepening of Jung's findings in the same area. It will, I believe, help to arrive at a typology differentiating people between mother-centered and father-centered characters, both with their particular history and their specific virtues and vices. It may show that instead of Freud's purely fatherly superego, there is a motherly conscience and a fatherly conscience, and that full maturity consists in the synthesis of both consciences, after they have been divorced from the persons of father and mother, and built up by the motherly and fatherly powers in each person.

Beyond that, Bachofen's findings will contribute to new insights in the field of psychopathology. One might discover that the mother-centered person suffers from certain forms of mental illness different from the father-centered person; a new light may be thrown on depressions, on certain forms of character neurosis of the receptive type on the one hand, and of obsessional neurosis and paranoia on the other. As one who has himself tried to apply, in a most limited way, Bachofen's findings to the problems of anthropology and psychology, I can only state that in my opinion the wealth of suggestions contained in Bachofen's work has not even begun to be touched.

17

Not that I believe that all his theories were correct. The history of ideas is the history of errors, and Bachofen is no exception to this rule. But what matters is the kernel of truth in an idea, and the fruitfulness of this very kernel for future thought. In this respect, Bachofen is one of the most fruitful and most advanced thinkers.

# 2

## The Theory of Mother Right and
## Its Relevance for Social Psychology (1934)

Bachofen's *Mother Right*, first published in 1861, shared a remarkable destiny with two other scholarly publications that appeared about the same time: Darwin's *Origin of Species* and Marx's *Critique of Political Economy* (both in 1859). All three works dealt with specialized scholarly disciplines, but they brought forth reactions from scholars and laymen far beyond the narrow confines of their own speciality.

As far as Marx and Darwin are concerned, this fact is obvious and calls for no further comment. The case of Bachofen is more complicated, for several reasons. First of all, the problem of matriarchy seems to have far less to do with matters that were vital to the maintenance of bourgeois society. Second, enthusiastic approval of the matriarchy theory came from two camps that were radically opposed to each other both ideologically and politically. Bachofen was first discovered and extolled by the Socialist camp—by Marx, Engels, Bebel, and others. Then, after decades of relative obscurity, he was again discovered and extolled by such anti-Socialist philosophers as

Klages and Bäumler. Over against these two extremes stood the official scholarship of the day, forming practically a solid front of rejection or outright ignorance—even among such representatives of the Socialist viewpoint as Heinrich Cunow. In recent years, however, the problem of matriarchy has played an ever-increasing role in scholarly discussions. Some agree with the matriarchal view, some reject it; almost all reveal the emotional involvement with the subject.

It is important to understand why the problem of matriarchy arouses such strong emotional reactions and how it is linked up with vital social interests. We also wish to uncover the underlying reasons why the matriarchy theory won sympathy from both the revolutionary and antirevolutionary camps. We can then see the relevance of this problem for the study of present-day social structures and their transformations.

One common element in the opposing attitudes to matriarchy is their common distance from bourgeois-democratic society. Such distance is obviously necessary if one wants to investigate and understand a social structure through the testimony of myths, symbols, legal institutions, etc.—certainly, if this society differs radically from bourgeois society not only in specific aspects but in its basic psychosocial traits. Bachofen himself saw this quite clearly. As he says in the Introduction:

"An understanding of matriarchal phenomena can be achieved only on one condition. The scholar must be able to renounce entirely the ideas of his own time, the beliefs with which these have filled his spirit, and transfer himself to the midpoint of a completely different world of thought . . . The scholar who takes the attitudes of later generations as his starting point will evidently be turned away from an understanding of the earliest time." (Bachofen, 1967, 81, 82)

Bachofen's prerequisite was certainly evident in those who

rejected their age—whether they looked back to the past as a lost paradise or looked forward hopefully to a better future. But criticism of the present was about the only thing that the two opposing adherents of the matriarchy theory did share. The sharp antagonism between the two groups on every other basic issue suggests that a variety of heterogeneous elements must have been at hand in both the matriarchy theory itself and the subject it dealt with. One group could focus on one aspect of the theory as the decisive element, the other group could focus on another aspect; in this way both could find reasons to advocate the theory.

Conservative authors like Bäumler looked backward to the past for their social ideals. What then were the reasons for their particular sympathy for the matriarchy theory? Engels gives one answer by pointing to—and criticizing—Bachofen's attitude in favor of religion, which Bachofen expresses himself clearly:

"There is only one mighty lever of all civilizations, and that is religion. Every rise and every decline of human existence springs from a movement that originates in this supreme sphere." (*Ibid.*, 85)

This attitude is certainly not typical of Bachofen alone. But it is of fundamental importance for his theory, which assumes a close connection between women and religious sentiment:

"If especially matriarchate must bear this hieratic imprint, it is because of the essential feminine nature, that profound sense of the divine presence which, merging with the feeling of love, lends woman, and particularly the mother, a religious devotion that is most active in the most barbarous times." (*Ibid.*)

Bachofen thus sees religious aptitude as the distinctive "disposition" of the female, and religion as a specific trait of matriarchy. Nor does Bachofen regard religion simply as a form

21

of cultic worship and consciousness. One of his most brilliant thoughts is his view that a given structure of the human psyche is related to a specific religion—although he turns the relationship upside down and derives the psychic structure from the religion.

The Romantic aspect of Bachofen's theory shows up even more clearly in his attitude toward the past: he directs his love and attention, in large measure, to the remotest past of mankind, which he idealizes. Even more significant, he sees respect for the dead as one of the most basic—and admirable—traits of matriarchal cultures. In his treatment of the Lycian matriarchy, he notes that "the whole life-style of a nation can be seen in its attitude toward the world of the dead. Worship of the dead is inseparable from respect for one's ancestors, and the latter is inseparable from love for tradition and a past-oriented outlook." (*Ibid.*, 92)

Deeply rooted in the maternal-tellurian mystery cults he finds "an emphatic accentuation of the dark, deadly side of nature's life, which is characteristic of the matriarchal outlook. Bäumler clearly points out the difference between the Romantic and the revolutionary outlook in this respect:

"If a person wants to understand myths, he must have a deep feeling for the power of the past. In like manner, if a person wants to understand revolutions and revolutionaries, be must have a profound awareness of the future and its potential.

"To understand the exact nature of this outlook, a person must clearly see that it is not the only possible conception of history. From a deep feeling for the future one may fashion another conception of history—one that involves active, masculine effort, conscious activity, and revolutionary ideals. In the latter framework, man stands free and unshackled in the present and creates the future out of nothing. In the former framework, man is enfolded in the whole "cycle of birth," in the transmission of blood-descent and time-honored customs; he is a member of some "Whole" that loses itself in the unknown recesses of the past . . . The dead will be there, if the living so resolve. They are not dead and gone forever from the earth. All one's ancestors still exist. They continue to advise and act in the community of their descendants." (Bachofen 1926, 112, 118)

In Bachofen's conception of the matriarchal psychic structure and the chthonic religion related to it, the decisive feature is the attitude of matriarchal society toward nature, its orientation toward material things as opposed to intellectual and spiritual realities.

"Matriarchy is bound up with matter and a religious stage of development that acknowledges only corporeal life . . .

"The triumph of paternity brings with it the liberation of the spirit from the manifestations of nature, a sublimation of human existence over the laws of material life. While the principle of motherhood is common to all spheres of tellurian life, man, by the preponderant position he accords to the begetting potency, emerges from this relationship and becomes conscious of his higher calling. Spiritual life rises over corporeal existence, and the relationship with the lower spheres of existence is restricted to the physical aspect. Maternity pertains to the physical side of man, the only thing he shares with the animals; the paternal-spiritual principle belongs to him alone. Here he breaks through the bonds of tellurism and lifts his eyes to the higher regions of the cosmos." (Bachofen 1967, 109–10)

Two traits, therefore, characterize the relationship of matriarchal society to nature: passive surrender to nature; and recognition of natural and biological values, as opposed to intellectual ones. Like the mother, nature is the center of matriarchal culture; and mankind ever remains a helpless child in the face of nature.

"In the former [i.e., matriarchal culture] we have confinement to matter, in the latter [i.e., patriarchal culture] we have intellectual and spiritual development. In the former we have unconscious lawfulness; in the latter, individualism. In the former we find abandonment to nature; in the latter we find exaltation above nature, a breaking of the old barriers, and the painful strivings of promethean life replacing the constant rest, peaceful pleasure, and eternal infantilism in an aging body. The mother's free giving is the exalted hope of the Demeter mystery, which is perceived in the fate of the grain-seed. Hellenic man, on the contrary, wants to win everything, even the most exalted heights, on his own. In struggle he becomes aware of his fatherly nature, and raises himself above maternalism to which he had once completely belonged, and struggles toward his own divinization. No longer does he look for the spring of immortality in the child-bearing woman; now he looks for it in the male-creative principle, on which he bestows the divinity that was once accorded only to motherhood." (Bachofen 1926, 49)

The value system of matriarchal culture fits in with this passive surrender to mother, nature, and earth and to their central role. Only the natural and biological are worthwhile; the spiritual, cultural, and rational are worthless. Bachofen developed this line of thought most clearly and completely in his concept of justice. In contrast with bourgeois natural law, where "nature" is patriarchal society turned into an absolute, matriarchal natural law is characterized by the dominance of instinctual, natural, blood-based values. In matriarchal law, there is no logical, reasonable balancing of guilt and atonement; it is dominated by the "natural" principle of the talion, of returning like for like.

This exclusive respect for the bonds of blood in matriarchal "natural law" is shown most impressively by Bachofen in his interpretation of Aeschylus' Oresteia. For the sake of her lover

Aegisthus, Clytemnestra slew her husband Agamemnon on his return from the Trojan War. Orestes, the son of Agamemnon and Clytemnestra, avenged this marital murder by slaying his mother. The Erinyes (or Furies), the ancient maternal goddesses who are now overthrown, pursue Orestes for his deed; on the other hand, he is defended by the new divinities of victorious patriarchy, Apollo and Athena, who sprang from the head of Zeus rather than from a mother's womb. What is the essential conflict here? For matriarchal law, there is only one crime: the violation of the blood bond. The Erinyes do not pursue the faithless wife because "she was not related by blood to the man she slew." Infidelity, however foul, does not concern the Erinyes. But when a person violates the ties of blood, no reasoned balancing of justifiable or excusable motivation can spare the doer from the merciless severity of the natural *lex talionis*.

Gynecocracy is "the realm of love and the blood-bond as opposed to the male-apollonian realm of consciously deliberated action." (Bäumler 1926, 233) Its categories are "tradition, generation, and living interconnectedness through blood and procreation." (*Ibid.*, 119) These categories are used in a concrete sense in Bachofen's work. They are removed from the realm of philosophical speculation and elevated to the realm of scholarly investigation into empirical, ethnological documents, thereby investing the latter with new weight. The vague concepts of nature and the "natural" way of life are replaced by the concrete image of the mother and an empirically demonstrable matricentric legal system.

Bachofen did not simply share the Romanticists' past-oriented and nature-centered outlook. He adopted one of the most fertile ideas of Romanticism as central to his work and developed it far beyond what it had meant in Romantic philosophy. This idea was the distinction between masculine and

25

feminine, which were seen as two qualities that were radically different, both in organic nature and in the psychic, spiritual, and intellectual realms. With this conception, the Romantics (and a few representatives of German Idealism) stood in sharp opposition to popular ideas that had been espoused in the seventeenth and eighteenth centuries—especially in France.

The central point of the earlier theories was summed up in the phrase "Souls have no sex." A whole series of books had examined the man–woman relationship, and the conclusion was always the same. Male and female did not represent qualities that were distinctively imbedded in the intellect and psyche. Whatever psychic differences were to be found between men and women were to be explained simply and solely in terms of their different training and education. It was this factor that made men and women different, even as it made one group different from another in social life.

This earlier notion about the fundamental sameness of the sexes was closely tied up with a political demand, which, made with varying degrees of intensity, played an important role in the era of bourgeois revolution. The demand was the emancipation of woman, her intellectual, social, and political equality. It is easy enough to see how theory and political cause dovetailed in this case. The theory that woman and man were identical formed the basis for demanding her political equality. But whether it was expressed or only implied, woman's equality meant that she, in her very essence, was the same as man in bourgeois society. Emancipation did not mean, therefore, that she was free to develop her specific, as yet unknown, traits and potentialities; on the contrary, she was being emancipated in order to become a bourgeois man. The "human" emancipation of woman really meant her emancipation to become a bourgeois male.

Along with a reactionary political development, there was a change in the theory of the relationship between the sexes and of the "nature" of man and woman. In 1793 women's clubs were shut down in Paris. The theory of basic psychic identity was replaced by the notion that there was a fundamental and unalterable "natural" difference between the sexes. With the later Romantics, the conception of the fundamental difference between maleness and femaleness was further elaborated by references to historical, sociological, linguistic, mythological, and physiological problems. In contrast to German Idealism and early Romanticism, the meaning of the word "woman" seems to have undergone a change. Whereas formerly "woman" signified her quality as lover, and union with her the experience of authentic "humanness," it came more and more to mean "mother," and the bond with her a return to "nature" and harmonious life in nature's womb.

The Enlightenment had denied sexual differences in the psyche, proclaiming the equality of the sexes, and equating human being with the bourgeois male. This theory was an expression of its efforts to grant social freedom and equality to women. Once bourgeois society had consolidated its gains and retreated from its progressive political positions, it no longer needed the notion of equality between the sexes. Now it needed a theory propounding the natural differences between the sexes, in order to have a theoretical basis for the demand for the social inequality of men and women. But while the new theory went deeper psychologically, its fine words about the dignity of woman, etc., merely served to maintain woman in her dependent position as man's servant.

I shall try to indicate later why and how a class society is so closely tied up with male rule over the family. But it should already be clear that any theory propounding the universal significance of sex differences would appeal very strongly to the champions of male, hierarchical class rule. Herein lies one of the important reasons why Bachofen won sympathy from the conservative camp. But it should be pointed out that Bach-

ofen himself largely overcame the potential reactionary interpretation of his theory by exploring the principle of the
differences between sexes in a radical way and by discovering
earlier social and cultural structures in which woman's superiority and authority were evident.

One essential feature of the Romantic conception is that the
difference between the sexes was not viewed as something that
was socially conditioned or had gradually developed in history;
it was supposed to be a biological fact that would never
change. Relatively little effort was made to establish the real
nature of masculine and feminine qualities. Some regarded the
character of the bourgeois woman as an expression of her "essence." Others pursued a superficial approach to the difference
between male and female: Fichte, for example, believed that
the whole difference was based on their "natural" difference
in behavior in the sex act.

The later Romantics equated "woman" with "mother," but
they also turned away from vague conclusions and began to
undertake empirical investigations of the motherly principle in
historical and biological reality. In so doing, they added extraordinary depth to the mother concept. Bachofen himself,
although to some extent sticking to the notion of the "natu-
ralness" of the differences between the sexes, also arrived at
important new insights. One was that woman's nature developed from her real "practice" in life—her early care of the
helpless infant, necessitated by the biological situation.

This fact, along with several others already mentioned,
should suggest that Bachofen was hardly a full-fledged Romantic, as Klages and Bäumler would have us believe. As we
shall see, the "blessed" matriarchal society of Bachofen contains many traits that reveal a close kinship with the ideals of
socialism. For example, concern for man's material welfare
and earthly happiness is presented as one of the central ideas

of matriarchal society. On other points, too, the reality of matriarchal society as described by Bachofen is closely akin to Socialist ideas and goals and directly opposed to Romantic and reactionary aims. According to Bachofen, matriarchal society was a primeval democracy where sexuality was free of Christian depreciation, where maternal love and compassion were the dominant moral principles, where injury to one's fellowman was the gravest sin, and where private property did not yet exist. As Kelles-Krauz points out, he characterizes matriarchal society by alluding to the old legend of the sumptuous fruit tree and the miraculous spring: both dried up when men converted them into private property. (Kelles-Krauz 1975, 522)

Frequently, though by no means always, Bachofen reveals himself to be a dialectic thinker. Note this remark: "In order to be comprehensible, the Demetrian gynecocracy demands the assumption of an earlier, cruder state of affairs that would have been directly opposed to the basic principles of the Demetrian way of life; the latter arose in a struggle against this earlier situation. Thus the historical reality of matriarchy is a testimony of the historical reality of hetaerism." (Bachofen 1926, 31) Bachofen's philosophy is akin to that of Hegel in many respects:

"The advance from the maternal conception of mankind to a paternal conception was the most important turning point in the history of the relationship between the sexes. . . . In the accentuation of paternity we have the deliverance of the human spirit from the phenomena of nature; in the successful implementation of paternity we have the elevation of human existence above the laws of corporeal life." (*Ibid.*, 48–49)

For Bachofen, the supreme goal of man's destiny is "the elevation of earthly existence to the purity of the divine father principle." He sees the victory of the paternal-spiritual principle over the maternal-material principle realized historically in the victory of Rome over the Orient—particularly over Carthage and Jerusalem:

"It was a Roman thought that spurred Europeans to put their stamp on the whole earth. The thought was simply this: that only the free rule of the spirit, not any physical law, determines the fate of peoples." (*Ibid.*, 571)

There is obviously a sharp contradiction between the Bachofen who admires gynocratic democracy and the aristocratic Bachofen of Basel who opposed the political emancipation of woman and who said: "By force of circumstances, democracy always paves the way for tyranny; my ideal is a republic ruled, not by the many, but by the best citizens." (Kelles-Krauz 1975, 522) It is a contradiction that crops up on several different planes. On the philosophical plane, it is the believing Protestant and Idealist against the Romantic; and the dialectic philosopher against the naturalistic metaphysician. On the social-political plane, it is the anti-Democrat against the admirer of a Communist-democratic social structure. On the moral plane, it is the proponent of Protestant bourgeois morality against the advocate of a society where sexual freedom reigned instead of monogamous marriage.

Unlike Klages and Bäumler, Bachofen makes no effort to harmonize these contradictions. The fact that he lets them stand is one reason he won such wide approval from those Socialists who sought not reform, but a thoroughgoing change of society's social and psychic structures.

The fact that Bachofen embodied such contradictions and scarcely tried to hide them is essentially due to the psychological and economic conditions of his personal existence. The breadth of his human and intellectual range was considerable, but his predilection for matriarchy apparently stemmed from his intense fixation on his own mother: he did not marry until he was forty, after the death of his mother. Moreover, his inheritance of ten million dollars permitted him to remain aloof from certain bourgeois ideals, and such aloofness was a necessity for any admirer of matriarchy. On the other hand, this patrician of Basel was so thoroughly rooted in his entrenched patriarchal tradition that he could not help but remain loyal to the traditional Protestant-bourgeois ideals. Neo-Romantics, such as Schuler, Klages, and Bäumler, saw only the Bachofen who propounded irrationalism, surrender to nature, and the exclusive rule of naturalist values based on the blood bond and earthly ties. They solved the problem of Bachofen's contradictions by adopting a one-sided interpretation of him.

The Socialists, too, recognized the "mystic" side of Bachofen, but they directed their attention and sympathy to Bachofen the ethnologist and psychologist—i.e., to that part of his work that accounts for his importance in the history of scholarship.

It was Friedrich Engels, more than anyone else, who made Bachofen's work known in the nineteenth century. In his *Origin of the Family, Private Property, and the State,* Engels asserts that the history of the family dates from Bachofen's mother right. Naturally, he criticizes Bachofen's idealist position, which derives social relationships from religion, but says:

"None of this, however, detracts from his groundbreaking work. He was the first to replace an unknown primeval state with a state of sexual intercourse unbound by rules. He did this by pointing out that ancient classical literature gives us many indications that monogamy was preceded by a prior state among the Greeks and Asians. In this prior state, not only did men have sexual relations with more than one woman, but women also had sexual relations with more than one man, without infringing against the mores. Furthermore, he has

31

shown us that the line of descent originally was traced only through the female line, from mother to mother, and that the exclusive validity of the female line of descent continued for a long time—even into the eras of monogamy when the knowledge of paternity was well established. This original position of the mother, in which she was the only sure parent of the child, ensured to mothers (and hence to women) a higher social status than they have ever had since then. Bachofen, to be sure, does not spell out these theses so explicitly, because his mystical outlook prevented him from doing so. But he did establish them, and this was a revolutionary step in 1861."

Sixteen years later, the American ethnologist Lewis H. Morgan demonstrated the existence of a matriarchal social structure in a very different area; and he used methods that were quite different from those of Bachofen. His book *Ancient Society* was thoroughly studied by Marx and Engels, and served as the basis for Engels's work on the family. Commenting on the matriarchal gens discovered by Morgan, Engels remarked that it had "the same significance for prehistory that Darwin's theory of evolution had for biology and that Marx's theory of surplus work had for political economy." There could be no higher praise from Engels, who went on to say: "The matriarchal gens have become the central point around which the whole science turns. We now know where to look, what to look for, and how to organize and group our findings."

It was not only Engels who was impressed by the discovery of matriarchy. Marx left behind a whole series of critical notes, which Engels utilized in his work. Bebel grounded his socialist best-seller, *Die Frau und der Sozialismus (Woman and Socialism)*, on the theory of matriarchate. Similarly, Marx's son-in-law, Paul Lafargue, wrote about the "awesome role of priestess and guardian of the mysteries that woman had in the primitive community" (Kelles-Krauz 1975, 6) and her attaining this role again in a future society. Kelles-Krauz asserted that Bachofen dug under the bourgeois renaissance and unearthed the precious seeds of a new revolutionary renaissance: the renaissance of the Communist spirit. (*Ibid.*, 524)

What accounts for the Socialists' favorable attitude toward the matriarchal theory? The first thing, as we noted earlier in connection with the Romantics, was their emotional and ideological distance from bourgeois society. Bachofen had pointed out the relativity of existing societal relationships. He had underlined the fact that monogamous marriage was not an eternal "natural" institution at all. Such a view could only be welcomed by a theory and political activity that advocated a fundamental change of the existing social structure. In Bachofen's own political position, this was a problematic aspect of his theory:

"The exclusivity of the marital bond seems so indispensable, so intimately tied up with the nobility of human nature and its lofty vocation, that most people regard it as the original state of affairs. The assertion that there were deeper, unfettered relations between the sexes is regarded as a dismally erroneous or useless speculation on the beginnings of human existence; so it is sloughed off as a bad dream. Who wouldn't like to adopt the common view, to spare our species from the painful memory of its shameful early days? But the evidence of history prevents us from giving in to the promptings of pride and egotism, from doubting the painfully slow progress of man toward higher marital morality." (Bachofen 1926, 30)

Aside from the fact that the theory of matriarchy underlined the relativity of the bourgeois social structure, its very special content could not but win the sympathy of Marxists. First of all, it had discovered a period when woman had been the authority and focal point of society, rather than the slave of man and an object for barter; this lent important support to the struggle for woman's political and social emancipation. The great battle of the eighteenth century had to be picked up afresh by those who were fighting for a classless society. In terms of its psychosocial foundations, the patriarchal social structure is closely bound up with the class character of present-day society. This society is based, to an important degree, on specific psychic attitudes that are partially rooted in unconscious drives; and these psychic attitudes effectively complement the external coerciveness of the governmental apparatus. The patriarchal family is one of the most important loci for producing the psychic attitudes that operate to maintain the stability of class society. (Cf. Fromm, 1932a)

Let me focus on the most important aspect. We are dealing here with an emotional complex that might well be called the "patricentric" complex. Characteristically, it includes the following elements: affective dependence on fatherly authority, involving a mixture of anxiety, love, and hate; identification with paternal authority vis-à-vis weaker ones; a strong and strict superego whose principle is that duty is more important than happiness; guilt feelings, reproduced over and over again by the discrepancy between the demands of the superego and those of reality, whose effect is to keep people docile to authority. It is this psychosocial condition that explains the family's almost universal regard as the foundation (or at least one of the important supports) of society; it also explains why any theoretical assault on the family, such as Bachofen's theory, would necessarily win the support of Socialist writers.

Of particular importance for our problem is the picture that Bachofen (as well as Morgan) gives of the social, psychic, moral, and political relationships characteristic of matriarchy. But while Bachofen looks back nostalgically toward this earlier societal stage and regards it as being gone forever, Morgan talks about a higher stage of civilization which is yet to come: "it will be a recurrence, but on a higher level, of the freedom, equality, and brotherhood characteristic of the ancient gens." Bachofen himself graphically describes these traits of freedom, equality, and brotherhood that were to be found in matriarchal society, whose governing principles are not anxiety and submissiveness, but love and compassion.

Bachofen's favorable reception among socialists was also helped by the decisive role of concern for man's material happiness on earth played in matriarchal society. Even though on the theoretical level, this naturalistic materialism, rooted in the mother's energy dedicated to the betterment of man's material life, is basically different from dialectic materialism, it contains an acceptable social hedonism that explains why it was so well received by the proponents of socialism.

Some general remarks seem to be in order concerning the principle of a complete lack of sexual restrictions, which Bachofen attributes to early gynocratic society. It would certainly be erroneous to maintain that restrictions in the sexual sphere are to be explained purely in terms of the existence and nature of class society, and that a classless society would necessarily restore the unlimited sexual relations described by Bachofen. On the other hand, we must say that a morality which deprecates and devalues sexual pleasure does perform an important role in maintaining a class society and that any attack on this morality, such as Bachofen's theory certainly was, would be a further reason for his favorable reception among the Socialists.

Sexuality offers one of the most elementary and powerful opportunities for satisfaction and happiness. If it were permitted to the full extent required for the productive development of the human personality, rather than limited by the need to maintain control over the masses, the fulfillment of this important opportunity for happiness would necessarily lead to intensified demands for satisfaction and happiness in other areas of life. Since the satisfaction of these further demands would have to be achieved through material means, these demands of themselves would lead to the breakup of the existing social order. Closely allied to this is another social function of restrictions on sexual satisfaction. Insofar as sexual pleasure as such is declared to be something sinful, while sexual desires remain perpetually operative in every human being, moral prohibitions always become a source of production for guilt feelings, which are often unconscious, or transferred to different matters.

These guilt feelings are of great social importance. They account for the fact that suffering is experienced as just punishment for one's own guilt, rather than blamed on the defects of the social organization. They eventually cause emotional intimidation, limiting people's intellectual—and especially their critical—capacities, while developing an emotional attachment to the representatives of social morality.

Let me add one final pertinent viewpoint. The clinical investigations of psychoanalytic individual psychology have been able to give us some indications that the suppression or acceptance of sexual satisfaction has important consequences for man's drives and character structure. (Fromm 1932a) The development of the "genital character" is conditioned by the absence of sexual restraints, which impede the optimal development of a person. Among the qualities undoubtedly belonging to the genital character is psychic and intellectual independence, whose social relevance needs no further emphasis. On the other hand, the suppression of genital sexuality leads to the development or intensification of such instinctual tendencies as the anal, the sadistic, and the latent homosexual, which are of decisive importance for the instinctual basis of present-day society.

Whatever the present status of matriarchy research, however, it seems certain that there are societal structures which can be called matricentric. And if we are to understand the social structures of the present day and their transformations, attention should be given to the present and future findings of this research.

The libidinal strivings of human beings are among the social "productive forces" in society. By virtue of their flexibility and changeability, they can adapt themselves considerably to the existing economic and social situation of the group—though there are limits to this adaptability. The psychic structure shared by the members of a social group represents an indispensable support for the maintenance of social stability. This structure, of course, is a support for stability only so long as the contradictions between the psychic structure and economic conditions do not go beyond a certain threshold; if this threshold is passed, the psychic forces tend to change or dissolve the existing order; it is important, though, to remember that the psychic structures of different classes can be radically different or even opposed to one another, depending on their function in the social process.

Although the individual is psychically different from the members of his own group, because of his individual constitution and personal life experiences—particularly those of early childhood—a large sector of his psychic structure is the product of adaptation to the situation of his class and the whole society in which he lives. Our knowledge about the factors determining the psychic structure of a given class or society, and hence about the psychic "productive forces" that are operative in a given society, is far less advanced than our knowledge about economic and social structures. One of the reasons for this is that the student of these problems is himself molded by the psychic structure typical for his society; accordingly, he comprehends only that which is like him. He easily makes the mistake of regarding his own psychic structure, or that of his society, as "human nature." He can readily overlook the fact that, under different social conditions, quite different drive structures have been and can be operative as productive forces.

The study of "matricentric" cultures is important for the social sciences. It not only brings to light psychic structures that are wholly different from those observed in our society, but at the same time, it throws new light on the "patricentric" principle.

The patricentric complex is a psychic structure in which one's relationship to the father (or his psychological equivalents) is the central relationship. In his concept of the (positive) Oedipus complex, Freud uncovered one of the decisive features of this structure—although he overestimated its universality because he lacked the necessary distance from his own society. The sexual impulses of the male infant, which are directed to his mother as the first and most important female "love-object," cause him to regard his father as a rival. This constellation acquires its characteristic significance from the further fact that in the patriarchal family the father simultaneously functions as the authority which governs the child's life. Quite apart from the physiological impossibility of the fulfillment of the child's wishes, the father's dual role has another effect that Freud pointed out: the child's desire to take the place of his father leads him to identify with his father to some degree. The child introjects the father, insofar as the latter is the representative of moral dictates, and this introjection is a powerful source for the formation of conscience. But since this process is only partially successful, the child's rivalry with the father leads to the development of an ambivalent emotional attitude. On the one hand, the child wants to be loved by his father; on the other hand, he more or less openly rebels against him.

However, the patricentric complex is also shaped by the psychic processes going on in the father himself. For one thing, he is jealous of his son. This is partly due to the fact that his lifeline is on the wane by comparison with that of his son. But an even more important cause of this jealousy is socially conditioned: it stems from the fact that the child's life situation is relatively free of social obligations. It is clear that this jealousy is greater where the weight of paternal responsibilities is heavier.

Still more important in determining the father's attitude toward his son are social and economic factors. Depending on economic circumstances, the son is either the heir to his father's estate or the future provider for his father in sickness and old age. He represents a sort of capital investment. From an economic viewpoint, the sums invested in his education and professional training are quite akin to those contributed toward accident insurance and old-age pensions.

Moreover, the son plays an important role insofar as the father's social prestige is concerned. His contributions to society and the concomitant social recognition can increase his father's prestige; his social failure can diminish or even destroy his father's prestige. (An economically or socially successful marriage by the son plays an equivalent role.)

Because of the son's social and economic function, the goal of his education is ordinarily not his personal happiness—i.e., the maximum development of his own personality; rather, it is his maximum usefulness in contributing to the father's economic or social needs. Frequently, therefore, we find an objective conflict between the son's happiness and his usefulness; but this conflict is usually not consciously noticed by the father, since the ideology of his society leads him to see both goals as identical. The situation is further complicated by the fact that the father frequently identifies himself with his son: he expects his son not only to be socially useful, but also to fulfill his own unsatisfied wishes and fantasies.

These social functions of the son play a decisive role in the quality of the father's love: he loves his son on the condition that the son fulfill the expectations that are centered around him. If this is not the case, the father's love can end, or even turn to disdain or hate. (This also accounts for the fact that the "favorite son"—the one who best fulfills his father's expectations—is a characteristic phenomenon in a patricentric culture.)

The conditional nature of paternal love typically leads to two results: (1) loss of the psychic security that comes from the knowledge that one is loved unconditionally; (2) intensification of the role of conscience—i.e., the person develops an outlook in which the fulfillment of duty becomes the central concern of life, because only that can provide some minimum guarantee of being loved. But even maximal fulfillment of the demands of conscience will not prevent guilt feelings from arising, because the person's performance will always fall short of the ideals set before him.

By contrast, a mother's love for the child is typically of a wholly different character. This is due, first and foremost, to the fact that a mother's love is completely unconditional in the first few years of her child's life. Mother's care of the helpless infant is not dependent on any moral or social obligations to be carried out by the child; there is not even an obligation to return her love. The unconditional nature of motherly love is a biological necessity which may also foster a propensity for unconditional love in the woman's emotional disposition. The certainty that mother's (or her psychological equivalent's) love is not dependent on any conditions means that the fulfillment of moral dictates plays a much smaller role, since it is not the condition for being loved.

The traits just described differ sharply from the image of the mother that is cherished in present-day patricentric society. Basically, this society only knows about courage and heroism on the part of the man (in whom the qualities are tinged with a large dose of narcissism). The image of the mother, on the other hand, has been a distorted one of sentimentality and weakness. In place of unconditional motherly love, which embraces not only one's own children but all children and all human beings, we find the specifically bourgeois sentiment of possessiveness injected into the mother image.

This change in the mother image represents a socially conditioned distortion of the mother-child relationship. A further consequence of this distortion—and also an expression of the Oedipus complex—is the attitude in which the desire to be loved by the mother is replaced by the desire to protect her and place her on a pedestal. No longer does the mother have the function of protecting; now she is to be protected and kept "pure." This reaction formation (distorting the original relationship to one's mother) is also extended to other mother symbols, such as country, nation, and the soil; and it plays an important role in the extremely patricentric ideologies of the present day. Mother and her psychological equivalents have not disappeared in these ideologies, but they have changed their function from protecting figures to figures in need of protection.

Summing up, we can say that the patricentric individual—and society—is characterized by a complex of traits in which the following are predominant: a strict superego, guilt feelings, docile love for paternal authority, desire and pleasure at dominating weaker people, acceptance of suffering as a punishment for one's own guilt, and a damaged capacity for happiness. The matricentric complex, by contrast, is characterized by a feeling of optimistic trust in mother's unconditional love, far fewer guilt feelings, a far weaker superego, and a greater capacity for pleasure and happiness. Along with these traits there also develops the ideal of motherly compassion and love for the weak and others in need of help.

41

While both types may well be found in any given society—depending primarily on the child's family constellation—it does seem that, as an average type, each is characteristic for a particular type of society. The patricentric type is probably dominant in bourgeois-Protestant society, while the matricentric type would play a relatively major role in the Middle Ages and in southern European society today. This leads us to Weber's treatment of the connection between bourgeois capitalism and the Protestant work ethos, in contrast to the connection between Catholicism and the work ethos of Catholic countries.

Whatever objections may be raised against specific theses of Weber, the fact of such a connection is now an assured part of scholarly knowledge. Weber himself treated the problem on the conscious and ideological level. But a complete understanding of the interrelationship can only be achieved by an analysis of the drive that serves as the basis for bourgeois-capitalism and the Protestant spirit.

While Catholicism also exhibits many patricentric traits—God the Father, hierarchy of male priests, etc.—the important role of the matricentric complex in it cannot be denied. The Virgin Mary and the Church herself psychologically represent the Great Mother who shelters all her children in her bosom. Indeed, certain maternal traits are ascribed to God himself—though not in a conscious way. The individual "son of the Church" can be sure of Mother Church's love, so long as he remains her child or returns to her bosom. This child relationship is effected sacramentally. To be sure, moral dictates play a major role. But a complicated mechanism operates to ensure that these dictates retain their necessary social weight while, at the same time, the individual believer can have the certainty of being loved without reference to the moral sphere. Catholicism produces guilt feelings in no small measure; at the same time, however, it provides the means for freeing oneself from these feelings. The price one must pay is affective attachment to the Church and her servants.

Protestantism, on the other hand, has done a thorough job of expurgating the matricentric traits of Christianity. Mother substitutes, such as the Virgin Mary or the Church, have disappeared, as have maternal traits in God. At the center of Luther's theology we find doubt or despair that sinful man can have any certainty of being loved. And there is only one remedy: faith. In Calvinism and many other Protestant sects, this remedy proves to be insufficient. It is complemented in a decisive way by the role assigned to the fulfillment of one's duty ("innerworldly asceticism") and by the necessity for "success" in secular life as the only proof of God's favor and grace.

The rise of Protestantism is conditioned by the same social and economic factors that made possible the rise of the "spirit" of capitalism. And, like every religion, Protestantism has the function of continually reproducing and strengthening the drive structure that is necessary for a particular society. The patricentric complex—in which fulfillment of duty and success are the major driving forces of life, while pleasure and happiness play a secondary role—represents one of the most powerful productive forces behind the enormous economic and cultural efforts of capitalism. Until the capitalist era, people (e.g., slaves) had to be compelled by physical force to dedicate every ounce of energy to economically useful work. Through the influence of the patricentric complex, people began to show the same total dedication of their own "free will," because the external compunction was now internalized. The internalization was effected most completely among the ruling classes of bourgeois society, who were the authentic representatives of the specifically bourgeois work ethos. In contrast to external force, however, the internalization process led to a different result: Fulfilling the dictates of conscience offered a satisfaction that contributed greatly to the solidification of the patricentric structure.

43

This satisfaction, however, was quite limited, because fulfillment of duty and economic success were poor substitutes
for traits now lost: the capacity to enjoy life and the inner
security derived from knowing that one is loved unconditionally. Moreover, the spirit of *homo homini lupus* led to personal
isolation and an incapacity for love—a heavy burden on the
psyche, which tended to undermine the patricentric structure,
even though the decisive factors operating to undermine the
structure were rooted in economic changes.

While patricentric structure had been the psychic driving
force behind the economic achievements of bourgeois-
Protestant society, at the same time it produced the conditions
that would destroy the patricentric structure and lead to a renaissance of a matricentric one. The growth of man's productive capacity made it possible, for the first time in history, to
visualize the realization of a social order that previously had
only found expression in fairy tales and myths, an order where
all men would be provided with the material means necessary
for their real happiness, with relatively little expenditure of
individual effort in actual labor, where men's energies would
be expended primarily in developing their human potential
rather than in creating the economic goods that are absolutely
necessary for the existence of a civilization.

The most progressive philosophers of the French enlightenment outgrew the emotional and ideological complex of the
patricentric structure. But the real, full-fledged representative
of the new matricentric tendencies proved to be the class
whose motive for total dedication to work was prompted basically by economic considerations rather than by an internalized compunction: the working class. This same emotional
structure provided one of the conditions for the effective influence of Marxist socialism on the working class—insofar as its
influence depended on the specific nature of their drive structure.

The psychic basis of the Marxist social program was predominantly the matricentric complex. Marxism is the idea that if the productive capabilities of the economy were organized rationally, every person would be provided with a sufficient supply of the goods he needed—no matter what his role in the production process was; furthermore, all this could be done with far less work on the part of each individual than had been necessary up to now, and finally, every human being has an unconditional right to happiness in life, and this happiness basically resides in the "harmonious unfolding of one's personality"—all these ideas were the rational, scientific expression of ideas that could only be expressed in fantasy under earlier economic conditions: Mother Earth gives all her children what they need, without regard for their merits.

It is this connection between matricentric tendencies and Socialist ideas that explains the "materialist-democratic" character of matriachal societies, which has led Socialist authors to express such warm sympathy for the theory of matriarchy.

# 3

## The Male Creation (1933)

It was Johann Jakob Bachofen, professor of Roman law in Basel, who presented the first major challenge to the naive beliefs that patriarchal society was a natural state of affairs and that man's superiority to woman was a self-evident matter. With a genius's insight, great acuity, and an extraordinary fund of knowledge, Bachofen plumbed the past and tore aside the veil the patriarchal spirit had cast over large and important areas of human history. In so doing, he revealed a picture of totally different societal forms and cultures, in which woman had played the leading role, in which she had been queen, priestess, leader; he brought to light societies in which only descent from the mother mattered, and the father was not recognized as a blood relation of his child. Bachofen believed that the matriarchy stood at the beginning of human evolution and that Father Right, the dominance of the male, prevailed only after a long historical process. He demonstrated that the difference between the male and female principles is a prevalent motive in all psychic life and that certain symbols express this difference: day–night, sun–moon, left–right.

Certainly Bachofen erred in a number of his individual assertions, but just as certainly later ethnological research corroborated a great many of his findings. He had discovered something crucial that pointed to new and fruitful paths to understanding the drives underlying social life, the difference between male and female nature, and the significance of the symbols representing this difference.

At first these paths were not pursued any further. For decades they disappeared almost entirely from sight. Except for a few kindred spirits of his day, Bachofen remained alone in his thinking. As a result of certain personal circumstances (his unusual intellectual gifts as well as an intense attachment to his mother) he came to understand the *relative* character of patriarchal society at a time when that society still stood at its zenith and did not yet regard itself as a problem. Consequently, Bachofen's theories did not gain the attention of contemporary thinkers and scholars or the more progressive members of the bourgeoisie.

The depths of psychic life, which Bachofen had sounded and brought to the surface again, were overlooked until Freud rediscovered them and was able to illuminate them far more extensively. His approach was entirely different from Bachofen's. Whereas the latter was a legal scholar, philologist, and Romantic who used myth, sculpture, and folk customs to support his theories, Freud was a physician and rationalist who utilized experiment, working with neurotics to prove by scientific method where the true springs of the psyche are to be sought and what their nature is. Only in one regard was Freud more a captive of the prejudices of his bourgeois-patriarchal society than Bachofen: in his overestimation of the role of the male and in his assumption of the male's natural superiority.

When the solid structure of patriarchal society began to give way, however, Bachofen's line of reasoning was destined to experience a renaissance. It was primarily a circle of German intellectuals that revived Bachofen's ideas—to be sure, in an eccentric and distorted manner, for it was a circle whose gaze was fixed exclusively on the past; its members had only scornful contempt for the present and no interest at all in the future. Grouped around an extraordinary teacher, its most important if not most profound representative was Ludwig Klages (1872–1956).

It took some time before ethnologists and psychologists could free themselves from patriarchal prejudices and, in the areas of individual as well as social psychology, approach the issue of Mother Right and reach an unbiased appraisal of the female psyche and its significance for the male. Among ethnologists the names of Briffault and Malinowski should be mentioned here and among psychoanalysts especially the name of Georg Groddeck, who was probably the first to note one of the most important phenomena in this area: the male's envy of the female and particularly his "pregnancy envy"—envy of the female's capacity to give birth, that natural productiveness denied him.

The work of Karen Horney tends in the same direction, exposing Freud's one-sided masculine standpoint and demonstrating the far-reaching psychological effects of bisexuality as well as the specific characteristics of fundamentally female sexuality. Groddeck's discovery of the male's envy of pregnancy was a finding of extraordinary significance. To be sure, in the course of cultural evolution conscious esteem for the female's natural productiveness has diminished in men *and* women. There are various reasons for this. In the first place, economic ones in the narrow sense: the more primitive an economy is and the less technology and machines are used in the production of goods, the greater the value of human labor for the economy; the greater, too, the value of women as the providers to society of that human labor, its most significant means of production. To the degree that human labor declines in importance in the overall economy, the role of woman and the high esteem for her specific ability necessarily diminishes.

Another economic reason of a broader nature comes into play here. In a relatively primitive society based mainly on agriculture and animal husbandry, security and wealth do not depend primarily on technical and rational factors. It is nature's productive force—that is, the fertility of the soil, the effects of water and sunlight—that plays the decisive role in human life and death. The crux of the economy is the mysterious power of nature giving birth out of itself to ever new products essential for human life. Who possesses this mysterious power of natural productiveness? Only woman. She alone has this ability, which she shares with all of nature, with plants and animals, and on which life and human existence depend. Doesn't man have to appear to himself as someone who is handicapped, who lacks the most important and crucial "potency," the capacity for natural production? Doesn't he have to admire and envy woman to an extreme degree for this advantage?

His envy and admiration had to be all the greater the less significant the role of the male principle, procreation, seemed to be. It took long stretches of time before a connection was made between the sex act and pregnancy, before the belief that a woman gave life to a child by herself, without any external influence, was relinquished. In the idea of the Virgin Birth, found in so many myths and religions, including Christianity, we find this ancient belief still preserved. Even today, in many primitive tribes the real connection has not yet been discovered. This fact is not so surprising when we consider that long periods of time had to pass for human beings to understand that the growth of plants, of fruit and bulbs, did not proceed

49

"by itself" but that seeds were required for Mother Earth to bestow her riches, to understand that whoever sows, also reaps. Surely this discovery was not made by pure chance. When nature's bounty ceased to be adequate to satisfy human needs because of impoverishment of the soil, overpopulation, and climatic changes, humans were forced to seek a new way of life that would have an actively procreative influence on nature. This led them to plant and to plow, to domesticate and breed animals.

Natural productiveness was supplemented with rational productiveness—a procreative influence on matter. The course of evolution of human society is characterized by an increase in the importance of rational productivity. Technology and machines are the result of reason's growing impact on matter, which leads to an ongoing increase in productivity and the creation of new and useful goods, which add to the enjoyment of life.

The importance attached to the rational, procreative factor during those decades of the tumultuous development of technology, the discovery and appropriation of new lands, and the creation of new trade relations was so great that natural factors began to be undervalued just as they had been overvalued earlier. An unconditional, limitless influence was attributed to "mind," to the male procreative principle, an attitude expressing itself in the philosophy of idealism as well as in certain features of bourgeois rationalism and in the strictly patriarchal structure of society.

It is easy to understand that in times of the growing importance of rational factors in society (and such times are certainly not only "modern," just as modern technology is only one—although the most dramatic—expression of rational-procreative productivity) woman's specific ability—her natural productiveness—lost in esteem in the social consciousness, while man's rational-procreative potency gained. The male role thus appeared increasingly desirable in human consciousness, the female role increasingly irrelevant and worthless.

This assessment, a value judgment in the mind of society, is only on a conscious level, however. The unconscious reacts more "naturally." It is not deluded by the extent of rational-technical development, for it knows that only woman possesses the mysterious capability of natural productiveness, a profound closeness to nature and to life, and the ability to understand life processes directly and instinctively, an ability that once made women into visionaries, prophets, and leaders. It is also an ability that today makes them much stronger guarantors of life than men, who are far less stable and who love to play with death and destruction.

In the male unconscious there is still a recognition of woman's superiority and her natural productiveness; there is still envy of her power. And in the unconscious of woman there is pride in this power and a recognition that she is superior to man.

The document that most powerfully exemplifies an extremely male, patriarchal attitude is the Old Testament, the most important literary foundation for this attitude in European and American culture and the classic statement of the feelings and beliefs of a patriarchy that deems itself superior to women. It is not surprising that the subject of productiveness, the Creation itself, also finds an extreme male solution in its pages.

The reason the Old Testament exhibits such a one-sided, male character is that as the primary text of Jewish monotheism it represents a male victory over female deities, over the matriarchal remnants in the social structure. The Old Testament is the triumphal hymn of the victorious male religion, a song of victory commemorating the destruction of all traces of the matriarchy in religion and society.

"In the beginning God created the heaven and the earth.

And the earth was without form, and void [*tohu wa-bohu*]; and darkness was upon the face of the deep. And the Spirit [breath, wind, *spiritus*] of God moved upon the face of the waters [*Tiamat*, the sea monster in the Babylonian creation epic]. And God said, Let there be light: and there was light" (Genesis 1:1–3). These opening lines of the biblical creation myth represent the proclamation of male domination and superiority. It is easy for Europeans and Americans, who from earliest childhood are so accustomed to these words that they seem almost self-evident, to forget how paradoxical, how "against nature" this myth is. It is not a woman, a mother, who creates the world, who gives birth to the universe, but a man. And how does he create, how does he give birth? With his mouth, through the word: "God said, let there be . . ."— this is the magic formula that runs through the entire creation myth, the formula that introduces every new act of creation, every new birth.

Before we consider in detail the central point, the male creation, let us take a look at the excessively male character of the account just cited.

The first act of creation is the birth of light. Light is always and everywhere a symbol of the male principle (cf. Bachofen's thorough research on this point), and it can come as no surprise that this account of creation makes light the beginning of the world. Nevertheless, certain remnants of old primal views have not been eradicated completely even in this extremely male account of creation. One can see that God is still presented as lying upon the primeval Mother, but she is referred to only in symbolic terms and no longer as the Great Mother herself. The male God is celebrated as the sole creator, as creator through the word.

The same "unnatural" tendency that disparages woman and eliminates her role appears in even more undisguised and pronounced form in the second account of creation (Gen. 2:4ff.).

Whereas in the first account God created man in his own image—"male and female created he them," that is, still with a remnant of the ancient conception of a bisexual deity—in the second account only man is created at first, although remnants of old ideas have not been entirely eliminated here either. "But there went up a mist [water] from the earth, and watered the whole face of the ground. And the LORD God formed man [Adam] of the dust of the ground [*adama*], and breathed into his nostrils the breath of life; and man became a living soul" (Gen. 2:6–7). Thus, there is here too a primal Mother, the Earth, who is moistened by fresh water, the male principle, and from whose womb man issues. (The ocean is consistently a female symbol, whereas fresh water [rivers and rain] symbolizes the male inseminating principle.) Here again, however, the male God is the real creator. All traces of the prior ideas disappear entirely in that part of the account which now follows. After man has been created as the first human being, his needs are then provided for. "It is not good that man should be alone" (Gen. 2:18), God says. A deep psychological insight, to be sure, but seen and formulated wholly from the standpoint of the male.

First the animals are created and offered to the man as "an help meet." But "for Adam there was not found an help meet for him" (Gen. 2:20). (Worth noting is the importance that the myth assigns to the man's giving of names: "And out of the ground the LORD God formed every beast of the field, and every fowl of the air; and brought them unto Adam to see what he would call them: and whatsoever Adam called every living creature, that was the name thereof" [Gen. 2:19]. We will come back to this point later.)

After the animals have proved to be useless in assuaging Adam's loneliness, woman is created: "And the LORD God caused a deep sleep to fall upon Adam, and he slept: and he took one of his ribs, and closed up the flesh instead thereof;

and the rib, which the LORD God had taken from man, made he a woman, and brought her unto the man. And Adam said, This is now bone of my bones, and flesh of my flesh: she shall be called Woman [*ischa*], because she was taken out of Man [*isch*]" (Gen. 2:21–23).

In the second account of the creation of woman, the paradox of the man giving birth is presented in a much more unequivocal and less veiled fashion than in the previous section of the myth. Nature has been turned upside down. It is not the woman who gives birth, not she who carries the child in her womb; it is the man who brings the woman into the world. It is he who gives birth, his chest serving as the uterus.

Hostility toward woman, fear of her—in short, an extremely male point of view—forms the salient character of the following account of the Fall of Man. Here we find ourselves totally within the emotional sphere of the patriarchy. God, the strong father, has issued a prohibition. He wants to show kindness to his son, man; he grants him woman and life in paradise, providing that Adam does not eat of the fruit of the tree of knowledge. God gives no reason for this prohibition, but he threatens death as punishment if Adam violates it. The real reason is given us by the snake: "For God doth know that in the day ye eat thereof, then your eyes shall be opened, and ye shall be as gods, knowing good and evil" (Gen. 3:5). Thus, what Adam must not do is identify with God; the son is not permitted to be the father. The forbidden apple, which Adam then eats, is a symbolic expression of the same idea. The forbidden fruit stands for the mother, for the maternal breast perhaps, and the prohibition against eating it is the prohibition against sexual relations with the mother.

In other words, we are confronted here with the classic Oedipus tragedy: the father forbids the son, under threat of death, to identify with him and to possess the mother. The son is disobedient, yet the threat is not carried out. He does not die, but he must leave paradise. What does life in paradise signify? It is the life of the infant at the mother's breast. In paradise the son didn't need to work; he didn't need to till the soil; he didn't need to provide himself with clothing. He was protected and nourished by the giving, kind, loving mother—by the fruitful earth. The father was not jealous as long as the son remained an infant and didn't become his rival. But when the son grows up, wants to be the father, desires the mother, he must then separate from her, must renounce her love and protection; he must search for nourishment himself, make his own clothes, engage in the struggle for existence.

The "Fall of Man," the expulsion from paradise, is a portrayal of the Oedipal conflict, of the transformation of the infant into the boy who identifies with the father, a portrayal of the introduction of the incest taboo by the father as a result of his son's growing up. We are certainly not dealing here with a myth that depicts the beginnings and the foundation of human history. Rather, it is the myth of the victorious patriarchal order of society and religion, and the Oedipal conflict as described by this myth is the classic conflict within the patriarchal family.

Everything is seen here from the perspective of the victorious male and pater familias. The woman is dangerous; she is the evil principle, and the man stands in fear of her. "And when the woman saw that the tree was good for food, and that it was pleasant to the eyes, and a tree to be desired to make one wise, she took of the fruit thereof, and did eat, and gave also unto her husband with her; and he did eat" (Gen. 3:6). The woman lacks self-restraint, is sensual and reckless; she seduces the man with her desire, which he cannot resist. As a result, he meets with disaster. There is probably no document that expresses more clearly and dramatically man's fear of woman and his accusation that she is a seductress who brings ruin than does this myth embodying the male, patriarchal worldview. From the Fall to the witch trials to Otto Weininger's thesis (1903) concerning the psychological and moral inferiority of woman, it is always the same contempt, hatred, and fear of woman that is typical of men in a patriarchal society.

The curse with which God sends his children out into the world also is in keeping with this same male attitude. The son must work; he will no longer live like the infant at the mother's breast. God says to the woman: "I will greatly multiply thy sorrow and thy conception; in sorrow thou shalt bring forth children; and thy desire shall be to thy husband, and he shall rule over thee" (Gen. 3:16). Can the patriarchal worldview be more plainly delineated than this? Here the man takes his revenge. His desire for the woman brought him disaster; now her desire shall bring her subjugation by the male. (In the patriarchal family the man, whether legitimately or not, can of course have as many women as he wishes, but the woman must be faithful to him; that is, for her libidinal satisfaction she is dependent on the only sexual object allowed her, whereas the male demonstrates his independence through sexual freedom and thereby ensures his dominance over the female.)

Especially characteristic is the part of the curse concerning childbearing. What the man sees, at least consciously, is not the joy of giving birth but solely the pain associated with it. This portion of the biblical myth is another classic instance of the typically male attitude toward giving birth. But does the situation appear the same in his unconscious? Is it not instead a reactive response that he sees only the negative, painful aspects of childbearing and not the mother's great joy? Isn't it his own deeply repressed pregnancy envy, his specifically male resentment, that makes him want the woman to pay with increased pain for her great advantage, for the natural productiveness he can never attain? Isn't it a consolation for his inability to give birth that it is a painful process and therefore not at all desirable?

We can better recognize the excessively male-patriarchal attitude of the biblical creation myth if we compare it to the Babylonian one that preceded it. A comparison will be especially helpful in clarifying a problematic feature of the myth—the male creation, creation through the word.

The Babylonian epic of creation, which was written most probably at the time of the Hammurabi dynasty (c. 2000 B.C.), has a specific political motivation: the political capital, Babili (Babylon), was also to be made the religious center of the land, with the patron god of Babylon, Marduk, becoming the supreme god of the entire land. The creation myth has the function of validating Marduk's claim to dominance by showing his place in the history of the gods and humankind. But this installation of a supreme male god as ruler of the world is carried out in a far less radical and encompassing way than in the Bible. The other male deities are not deposed and replaced by Marduk, nor is the tradition of the Great Mother, who presided over the world's beginning, eliminated.

The Babylonian myth too is the expression of a male patriarchal religion and societal order but one in which far more matriarchal traces remain than in the Old Testament and which therefore provides an extremely valuable complement to it. "There were many places where the ever-new creative and productive force of nature continued to be worshipped in the form of the mother goddess, now by one name, now by another. Thus, Ninkhursag or Mama was the chief goddess of Kesh; in Adab the same female principle was worshipped as the goddess Ninmah, in Hallab as Ishtar, in Akkad as Anunit, in Kish as Inanna, in Isin as Ninkarrana, in Uruk as Nana, etc; in Uruk the cult of the goddess forced that of the sky god Anu, whose daughter she was believed to be, completely into the background." (Ungnad 1921, 13)

How does the Babylonian myth begin?

When heaven above had not yet been named,
And the earth below did not have a name;
When primeval Apsu, begetter of all,
Tiamat, mother of all, and Mummu, their son,
Still mingled their waters;
When there was no solid ground nor marshland;
When none of the other gods existed,
Had not been called by name, their destinies not fixed;
It was then the gods were created by Apsu and Tiamat.*

Here it is not the male god who creates the world; rather, the world is the offspring of two primeval powers, the male and female principles: Apsu (fresh water) and Tiamat (ocean). The primordial sea (Tehom), also referred to in the biblical myth but not in the form of a goddess placed by the side of a male god, is still portrayed here as female, as the primeval mother who gives birth to gods and humans.

"The times grew and became long." Apsu and Tiamat give life to divine sons, gods who become increasingly proud and clever. Eventually they revolt against the mother:

*Trans. note: Because different translations of the Babylonian myth vary significantly in their interpretation, we have translated Ungnad's German version (see above), which is the one used by Erich Fromm. On occasion we have drawn on the English version by Alexander Heidel (*The Babylonian Genesis: The Story of Creation*, 2nd ed. [Chicago & London: University of Chicago Press, 1942 and 1951; Phoenix Books, 1963] ). We also consulted Joseph Campbell, *The Masks of God: Occidental Mythology* (New York: Viking Press, 1964).

The divine brothers joined together.
They disturbed Tiamat, scoffing at Apsu, their keeper.
They made Tiamat confused;
Now suddenly her omnipotence was gone!

Apsu was filled with sorrow;
Tiamat was distressed, troubled was her heart.
Mighty Mummu smote his thigh,
For their sons' doings were not good: they were planning
    rebellion!

Then Apsu, begetter of the great gods,
Called Mummu, his vizier, and said:
"Mummu, my vizier, my heart's delight,
Come, let us seek Tiamat!"

They went and, bowing before Tiamat,
Held counsel concerning the gods.
Opening his mouth, Apsu spoke these words,
Addressing Tiamat, the radiant goddess:

"Their doings are a boundless burden to me;
By day I cannot rest, by night I cannot sleep;
I want to destroy them, put an end to their doings,
That silence be restored and we find rest!"

When Tiamat heard his words,
She was wroth and shrieked
With anger and pain. Overwhelmed with rage,
She quickly devised an evil plan:

"What is left for us to do? To bring about their ruin!
We must hinder their actions, that we may reign forever!"

Then Mummu spoke, counseling Apsu,
And harsh was his advice:
"If their actions offend thee, then confound them,
That thou canst rest by day and sleep by night!"

When Apsu heard this, his face lighted up
At the wicked plan against his children.
He embraced Mummu, fell upon his neck,
Drew him close and kissed him.

In the narrative that follows, the sky gods are filled with great fear when they learn that the powers of chaos are going to attack them. Only one god knows what to do; it is Ea, the cleverest among them, who has the ability to vanquish all evil forces with incantations. He succeeds in slaying Apsu and fettering Mummu; Tiamat, however, remains unvanquished and with her a number of lower powers, who are mentioned now for the first time. One of them, Kingu, "the radiant god," turns out to be particularly stalwart. He urges Tiamat not to abandon her plan but to renew her struggle against the gods. Tiamat does not resist his encouragement for long: she gathers together her minions, who now set off for battle in a ghastly procession:

They gathered, then strode at Tiamat's side;
Furious, they plotted, not resting day or night;
Armed for battle, enraged and frenzied,
Boldly they banded together, ready to fight.

Tiamat, mother of chaos, who fashioned all things,
Gave out weapons, bringing to life giant serpents
Sharp and merciless of tooth;
With poison, not blood, she filled their bodies.

Raging dragons dreadful to behold
And of fearful force she brought to life.
Who looked upon them must perish from fright.
Their rearing bodies none could withstand.

She led into battle vipers, basilisks, and monsters,
Mad dogs, cyclones, and scorpion-men,
storm-demons, fish-men, and sea-rams.
Bearing fierce weapons, they knew no fear.

In full command was Tiamat, not brooking dissent.
Eleven kinds of creatures she sent into battle!
Among the host of the gods, her offspring,
She exalted Kingu, granting him power.

Clothing him in majesty, she entrusted all to his hand:
To march at the head of her army, to direct her forces,
To initiate combat, to launch the attack,
The leadership and high command of the battle.

"Ordained through magic, thou art now elevated;
Dominion over all the gods have I given thee!
Exalted be thou, my chosen spouse!
Mayest thou be extolled by the gods of the deep."

She placed on his breast the tablet of destiny, saying:
"May thy command be unwavering, thy words be
    binding!"

And Kingu, exalted, ruling now as supreme god,
Proclaimed to the gods, Tiamat's offspring, their destiny:
"Open your mouths to quell the flames!
Who proves himself brave will gain in power!"

How different this struggle and this revolt from the one described in the Bible, where the son is seduced by the woman and revolts against the father, who punishes him with expulsion from paradise, with separation from the mother. In the Babylonian version, the sons revolt against the primordial mother, who proves to be stronger than her husband. Apsu is overpowered, but Tiamat remains unvanquished. She is the terrifying warrior who places a male god, Kingu, in charge of her forces and makes him her consort, an action that reflects a characteristic found frequently—and only—in matriarchal societies: military and political leadership is in the hands of men, but they receive their authority and position from women and function only as their delegates.

Now two male gods—Ea and, after him, Anu—attempt to visit Tiamat and her consort Kingu. Anshar tells his son Anu to calm them with a magic spell:

> Anu obeyed the words of his father;
> He set out on his way to find Tiamat.
> But when he drew nigh, perceiving her intent,
> All resistance left him. He retreated!

Then Anshar and Ea turn to the god who is to become the hero of this epic, Marduk. He is confident of victory and says to Anshar:

> "Has ever a man opposed thee?
> Should now a woman, Tiamat, attack thee?
>
> O father of the gods, be glad and rejoice;
> For soon thy foot shall rest on Tiamat's neck!"

The gods assemble to name Marduk the warrior who will fight against Tiamat. But before he is ultimately made ruler and leader, he must undergo a test to prove he is capable of vanquishing the mighty Tiamat:

> They placed a garment in their midst,
> Addressing Marduk, first among them:
> "May thy destiny, O lord, be supreme among the gods.
> If thou commandest destruction and creation, may it be
>      so!
> At thy order, may the garment disappear;
> Command again, and may it reappear!"

> Marduk gave the command, and behold, the garment
>      disappeared!
> Again he commanded, and the garment reappeared!

> When the gods beheld the force of his word,
> They rejoiced and gave homage, saying, "Marduk is
>      king!"
> They bestowed on him scepter, throne, and staff,
> Also a victory weapon to smite the foe, saying:
> "Go now, put an end to Tiamat's life.
> Let the winds bear her blood to secret places."

We shall come back to the details of this crucial test, but first I want to describe the outcome of the battle. Marduk makes a net in which to catch Tiamat; he calls up seven storms to "trouble Tiamat within." With these weapons—in the winds we again recognize a typically male symbol—he sets out against Tiamat. Then he encounters her:

> As he gazed, Marduk grew confused; he wavered.
> Forgotten was his resolve and faltering his action.

Tiamat stood her ground. Not turning her head,
She hurled her venom at him with her full lips.

But Marduk takes heart. Although he at first loses his position of superiority, it is now Tiamat who loses her self-confidence. Marduk challenges her to battle, crying:

"Do thy utmost! Secure thy weapons!
Lay on! Let us two do single combat!"

When Tiamat heard these words,
She was beside herself and lost all reason.
Full of wrath and rage, she shrieked,
Trembling violently from head to foot.

She cast a magic spell, murmuring incantations
While the gods of battle prepared their weapons.

Tiamat and Marduk advanced toward each other;
They pressed on, approaching for combat.
But the lord cast his net and caught her in it;
He let Evil Wind, his servant, loose in her face.

When Tiamat opened her mouth to devour him,
Evil Wind flew in, and her lips could not close.
With raging winds Marduk filled her body
Till she lost her senses, her mouth still open wide.

He shot an arrow, ripping open her body;
It tore her inner parts, piercing her heart.
He subdued her, putting an end to her life,
Threw down her corpse, and trod upon it.

After he had slain Tiamat, the leader,
Her forces broke up, her minions dispersed.
The gods, her helpers, who had marched at her side,
Turned back, trembling and quaking.

They tried to escape, in fear for their lives,
But Marduk ensnared them; they could not flee!

He bound them all and smashed their weapons.
They sat enmeshed, caught in his net.
The spheres resounded with their lamentations.
Confined as prisoners, they received their punishment.

The eleven kinds of creatures dread of mien,
The diabolical brood that had marched with Tiamat,
He cast into fetters, destroying their power.
Despite their resistance, he trampled them down.

As for Kingu, who had risen far above them,
Marduk subdued him, counting him among the dead gods,
And took from him the tablet of destiny, not Kingu's by
    right;
He marked it with his seal and placed it on his breast.

When Marduk had quelled and conquered his opponents,
Had completely defeated the fearful foe;
When he had gained victory for Anshar,
Had also fulfilled Ea's wish;
When he had tightly bound the captive gods;
The hero went to Tiamat, whom he had just subdued.

The lord trod on her remains;
With his terrible club he split her skull.

65

He cut into pieces the arteries of her blood,
Let the north wind bear her blood to secret places.

When the fathers saw this, they shouted with joy;
Gifts and offerings they sent to Marduk.

Then the lord paused, beholding her corpse;
He divided the heap, planning wisely:
Splitting her in two like a mussel,
Half of her he set in place to form the sky.

He put up a barrier, posting guards to watch over her,
And gave orders not to let her waters escape.
Striding across the heavens, he viewed the regions.
He approached the ocean, the dwelling of Ea.

The lord now took measure of the ocean;
He made the earth in the same proportions,
Calling it Esharra, which he built like the sky.
There he made abodes for Anu, Enlil, and Ea.

It is not difficult to recognize the symbolic significance of
the battle described here between Marduk and Tiamat. Their
struggle represents the sex act. Whereas the male becomes un-
sure of himself when he first sees the female, it is the female
who "loses her reason," who is beside herself when the real
struggle begins. She opens her mouth to devour him, but he
fills her body with raging winds, whereupon she loses her
senses. With her mouth still wide open, he shoots an arrow
into her and subdues her, "putting an end to her life." The
winds and the arrow are without doubt symbols for the male
genitals, just as the mouth symbolizes the vagina. The male's
fear of the female genitalia clearly takes the form of his fear

of being devoured by her, but in the end the male is the victor, having subdued and slain the female.

This description is familiar to the analyst. It portrays the sex act as a struggle, as a sadistic and bloody attack by the man upon the woman and also as the woman's attempt to kill the man during the sex act. The entire episode is presented from the perspective of the man, who succeeds here in subduing the dangerous woman and becoming the victor.

After Marduk's victory a new creation takes place. Splitting Tiamat's body in two, he creates the heavens from her corpse. Here, what is created is no longer the offspring of man *and* woman, but neither is it the work of man alone. Although he is the creator, he nevertheless needs the maternal body as his material.

After Tiamat has been slain and her helpers conquered, peace reigns between the gods and Marduk's creation, Man, whose main purpose in life will be to serve the gods.

Marduk speaks to the gods:

"Blood will I collect and also bones;
Then will I put together a being: Man shall be his name.
Yes, I shall create him, this being,
And it will be his duty to serve the gods.

The ways of the gods I will wisely alter.
They shall be divided into two groups, both honored
    alike."

Ea replied, responding thus,
Proposing a plan to please the gods:

"One of their brothers should be delivered up;
Let him be destroyed that you may create Man!

Let the great gods come together;
Then shall he be delivered up, and the rest may live."

The great gods were summoned by Marduk.
Walking among them, he gave his instructions,
And the gods listened to the words he spoke.
Thus did he address them:

"Verily, what I told you before has come to pass!
I speak the truth straight from my heart.
Who was it provoked the strife,
Luring Tiamat into war?

Let him who created the strife be delivered up;
Let him be punished for his offense."

The gods then gave their answer
To the king of the world, their lord and counselor:
"Kingu it was who provoked the strife,
Luring Tiamat into war!"

Kingu was bound and led before Ea;
His arteries were cut open as punishment!
With his blood was Man created.
The other gods King Marduk set free.

In gratitude for being set free, the gods pledge to erect a splen-
did temple in Marduk's honor. Marduk designates Babylon as
the site for this holy shrine. After the temple has been com-
pleted, Marduk invites all the gods to a meal there. Singing his
praises, the divine assembly pays tribute to him, the savior and
creator of worlds. Let's listen to the last verses. After Marduk
has been extolled as the god of "the good breath" and "holy incantations," the fifty names of Marduk are enumerated:

The aged should hold [his names] in remembrance and
    teach them;
Scholars and sages should give them wise consideration!
Let fathers instruct their sons;
May the ears of shepherds and herdsmen be opened to
    them.

Let Man rejoice in Marduk, the ruler of the gods;
May his land be fruitful and it go well with him.

Faithful is Marduk's word, infallible his utterance;
The commands from his mouth no god can alter.
Without fear is his gaze, neither wavering nor turning
    away;
When he is wroth, no god can withstand him.

Generous is his heart and great is his goodness;
Transgressor and sinner are given his blessing.

The epic ends on a note that is strongly reminiscent of the
Old Testament and its version of creation. A powerful, paternal, infallible, stern but also merciful and forgiving god rules
over the world. The merciful God, who possesses the fullness
of life, creates man, the work of his hands. He no longer creates jointly with woman or even from the woman's body; he
creates independently, albeit from the flesh and blood of a living being, of a god who must die so that humans may live.

Even though certain aspects of the conclusion of the Babylonian myth are reminiscent of the biblical account of creation,
it differs significantly both in the way it ends and in the nar-
ration as a whole.

In the Bible the male, paternal God stands alone as the single
victor and ruler. Not only are there no longer other gods beside
or beneath him, but the fact that he fought and conquered

earlier gods is completely omitted from the myth. Furthermore, only the primeval ocean, Tehom, is left to remind us of Tiamat, once recognized as the primal mother and ruler, and only Eden's serpent, which before its degradation was a royal animal, a mighty dragon, reminds us that the male god once had to battle against the giant serpents and raging dragons whom Tiamat engaged to fight for her.

The Babylonian epic has a far more conciliatory ending than the biblical one. To be sure, Tiamat, who represents matriarchal principles, is slain, and her husband and champion Kingu is destroyed, but Marduk pardons Tiamat's other allies, the Anunnakis, who then build a temple in honor of the victorious god. Marduk allows them to go on living as "gods of the underworld," and they are accepted into the hierarchy he heads as subordinate gods who serve him.

The Babylonian epic comes from a time when a male, paternal god gained supremacy over the entire world. But his victory was not so radical or so violent that it obliterated all memory of the former female goddesses and their male allies. They were still able to exist as deities of a lower order, and that is why it was possible for the Babylonian account to retain reminiscences that the Hebraic story ruthlessly expunged—traces of the struggle between two religious and societal orders, between the old matriarchal, maternal-chthonian religion characterized by night, water, and matter, and the new paternal religion characterized by light, wind, and spirit. The Babylonian epic stops where the biblical one begins; it tells of a battle, whereas the Bible tells only of a victory so total that the name of who was conquered and the fact that the battle took place are omitted. In this regard the Babylonian account is very similar to Bachofen's pioneering interpretation of the battle of the Erinyes against Apollo, god of light, and the ensuing outcome that makes them goddesses of a lesser rank in his service.

Let us now return to the question of the creation, specifically the male creation. In the Babylonian epic we encounter three different types of creation. To begin with, we find man and woman, fresh water and ocean, procreator and mother, who together give birth to gods; here we have creation that corresponds exactly to the conditions of nature, where male and female are dual creators. The older concept, according to which the female creates the world by herself and the great primordial mother stands alone at the beginning of all life, is no longer to be found in this account, for it originated in a matriarchal society, which obviously existed so long before the time in which the Babylonian epic was set down that there is no place for it anymore. The only remnant of the old matriarchal way of thinking is found in the fact that Tiamat is portrayed as the true queen and ruler, who at first remains unvanquished whereas her spouse Apsu is vanquished. She then names Kingu as her consort and the leader of her forces; yet her sons fear and respect *her*, not her husband.

We encounter the second type of creation after Tiamat's death when Marduk forms the heavens from her body. Here the natural realm is left behind. What is created is no longer the female's child, begotten by the male; it is produced by the male, yet the matter used is the female body. Although still the product of both female and male, it is now no longer the result of the sequence found in nature: insemination and pregnancy.

The third type of creation found in the Babylonian myth is Marduk's creation of man from the flesh and blood of the slain Kingu. The participation of the female has been completely erased. She does not give birth, nor is her body used as matter: the male god is the sole creator here. The natural sequence has been turned upside down and denied more radically than in the previous type of creation. But the male still depends on living matter, on flesh and blood that already exist. He is not the sole and absolute creator.

71

This type of creation corresponds entirely to the creation of woman as described in the Bible. Here too the male god creates a new being without the help of woman and is dependent on living matter that already exists. The biblical story is slightly more radical because it reverses nature even more thoroughly by portraying the male not only as the mother of man but even of woman herself.

Although one extreme is missing from the Babylonian myth—the parthenogenetic creation, creation by the female alone without help from the male—the other extreme is also missing: creation by the male alone, who doesn't need a living substance as his material, creation through the power of thought. This type of creation, depicted most vividly and graphically in the Greek myth of the birth of Athena from the head of her father, Zeus, is also encountered in the Bible. There, to be sure, the memory of the primeval mother Tiamat has not been completely erased and God is described as hovering over the waters, but the manifest meaning no longer assigns any essential role to the female element [the waters].

The biblical account does not begin, "In the beginning was chaos; in the beginning was darkness" but "In the beginning God created the heaven and the earth"—he alone, the male god, without the help and participation of the female. After an interruption of one verse, in which the old ideas still echo, the account continues, "And God said, Let there be light: And there was light" (Gen. 1:3). Here we can clearly see the extreme of a purely male creation, creation by the word alone, by thought, by spirit. No longer is the womb necessary for giving birth; no longer is matter necessary either. The mouth of the male, who speaks a word, has the ability to create life directly and with ease. What we find in the Bible is a concept that is the opposite of parthenogenesis, an extreme concept expressing an equally extreme patriarchal attitude that devalues and subjugates woman. The male appropriates that ability

72

which without any doubt belongs to woman alone: the ability to give birth, to create new life.

It must be remembered that this idea of creation by the spirit contradicts all natural and actual life processes to a far greater extent than does parthenogenesis. That the child is the product of both father *and* mother is a scientific truth that it took human beings a very long time to discover—the kind of fact that always has a theoretical quality to it, such as the fact that it is the Earth that revolves around the Sun and not the other way around. Although we know it is so, we *see* the Sun move; we *see* that the child comes from the mother, that it grows and moves inside her body, and that she then gives birth to it. On the other hand, we never see a direct connection between child and father, except in their resemblance. (This resemblance does not necessarily need to be associated with the act of creation even though once the male's role has been recognized, it serves as important and impressive evidence. This explains the Bible's emphasis on the child's resemblance to the father: "in the image of God created he him." [Gen. 1:27])

The thought that the male can create living beings by himself—with his mouth, through his word, out of his spirit—is the most unnatural fantasy conceivable; it denies all experience, all reality, every natural condition. It disregards all the laws of nature in order to attain the *one* goal of presenting the male as the perfect being per se, who possesses the ability life appears to have denied him, the ability to give birth. This fantasy, which can grow only in the soil of a one-sided, patriarchal society, is the archetype of all idealistic thinking that ignores natural circumstances and conditions. It is simultaneously an indication of the male's deep envy of the female, of his feeling of inferiority due to his lack of her ability to give birth, and of his desire to achieve this ability, even if by other means than hers.

In the Babylonian myth these two extreme methods of creation are missing: parthenogenesis as well as creation through the word, the purely male creation. But an event is described in the Babylonian myth that represents a kind of precursor to full-scale creation through the word and reveals in very clear fashion the real meaning of the male creation. It is the test Marduk must undergo before he is ultimately chosen to do battle against Tiamat—a test to assure the other gods that he will be victorious. What is the nature of this test? "They placed a garment in their midst, . . ." (see pp. 62–63).

It seems a strange test the hero must pass in order to prove he is suitable for the role he is to play. Whereas we would perhaps expect that he must prove his bravery or his cleverness, all that is required of him is to show that he can make a garment disappear and make it reappear by means of his word. What is the significance of this?

Marduk is supposed to fight against Tiamat. Should he be victorious, he could not be her inferior. But as a man he *is* inferior to her in one crucial point. Only she has the ability to create new life; only she can give birth, can bring things into being. It is she who gives life; it is also she who takes life away. The Great Mother is the kind, life-giving white mother, but she is also the deadly black mother, just as nature itself appears to human beings in this same dual aspect as both preserver and destroyer. (See in this connection Bachofen's comments on the dual significance of the figure of the mother as giver and taker of life.) If the male god is going to be able to triumph over the mother, he must compensate for his inferiority—his inability to give birth, to produce.

This, then, is the significance of the test. Marduk can do what the mother can. He can do what nature has denied the male. He can alter nature; he can make an object disappear and can make the same object reappear. It is clear that the object itself does not matter at all. It is a garment, an ordinary, everyday object. What does matter is that he, the male, is now no longer inferior to the female; he can create life and take it away just as she can. This is the meaning of the words of the myth:

When the gods beheld the force of his word,
They rejoiced and gave homage, saying, "Marduk is
    king!"

It is this test that shows Marduk to be Tiamat's equal, and it is this equality that guarantees his victory. The power of his mouth replaces the power of the female womb; the mouth of the male can give birth the way only the womb of the female can in reality.

In this test to which Marduk must submit we find the prototype of male creation, creation through the word. What is presented in the Babylonian myth only as a test of the male hero, becomes in the Biblical myth the method of creation of the world through the word. In the Bible God creates by means of the power of his word. Just as Marduk proceeds with the garment, so God proceeds with the cosmos. "And God said, Let there be light: and there was light" (Gen. 1:3). The male god has completely taken over the functions of the vanquished Great Mother. He can give birth, he can produce—with his spirit and his word he does away with the natural order of things; he alone rules.

This significance of the word appears only once again in the first chapters of Genesis when God brings all the animals "unto Adam to see what he would call them" (Gen. 2:19), and it is Adam who gives Eve her name: woman (*ischa*). The giving of names is a kind of second creation. Just as the male God first created living beings by means of his word, so too Adam creates them a second time by giving them names.

*—Translated by Hunter Hannum*
*and Hildegarde Hannum*

75

# 4

## Robert Briffault's Book on Mother Right (1933)

In his comprehensive work *The Mothers: A Study of the Origins of Sentiments and Institutions* (1928), Robert Briffault takes up the theme of Mother Right, for which Johann Jakob Bachofen and L. H. Morgan had established the theoretical basis in the 1860s and 1870s. For decades all reference to the theory of Mother Right disappeared from official scholarship, and the names of its originators were mentioned by only a few Socialist authors. In recent years a kind of renaissance has emerged among authors who represent a completely different Weltanschauung. The theory of Mother Right has been referred to and treated increasingly in scholarly as well as journalistic writings, and Briffault's book may well compel even those who until now have taken no notice of the subject to consider it.

But it would not be accurate if we added Briffault's book to the list of ethnological works dealing with Mother Right. It covers much more ground than that, belonging just as much to the disciplines of sociology and psychology as to that of ethnology. For the same reason it is also difficult to reduce the contents of his book to one main thesis. In any case, those critics err who maintain that Briffault's thesis does not go beyond demonstrating that more or less pronounced characteristics of Mother Right can be found to exist everywhere at the beginning of all societal evolution. Given the length of the book, many may well try to learn the main thesis from the title rather than from the content. But in fact the book is just as much about a psychology based on comparative ethnology and the history of marriage as it is about the theory of Mother Right. Briffault clearly states his point of departure in the Preface: starting with the question of the origin of social instincts he comes to the conclusion that it is to be found in maternal instincts. This leads him to examine those early stages in the evolution of society when societal organization and psychology were centered around the mother.

As important and numerous as the stimulating ideas are that Briffault provides concerning the general areas of sociology and social psychology, the greatest value of his book lies in its unusually rich material and many individual studies. Thus, the following remarks cannot claim to offer an exhaustive account of the book's content; they will simply give a few indications of Briffault's scholarly method and the focus of his research.

He begins by showing the pivotal part "traditional heredity" plays in the development of human cultural and emotional life. Biologically programmed instincts are transformed by social influences, and the variations among individuals within the various cultures are caused by the modifying effect of social conditioning. "Masculine" and "feminine" are for Briffault definitive psychological categories, but unlike the Romantics, he does not derive them from the "nature" of the two sexes but from the difference in the way they function in practical life.

With this shift he rescues the issue of sexual differences from the darkness with which natural philosophy had cloaked it and examines it in the light of scientific research.

Two crucial factors in the evolution of the feminine-maternal character, the *maternal instinct*, are the unusually long period of gestation in humans compared with the overwhelming majority of mammals and the protracted postnatal immaturity of the human child, which requires long-term care on the mother's part. Her instinct to care for her helpless child is responsible for the development of maternal love, which extends not only to the child, and certainly not only to her own child, but—in the form of social feeling, of altruism—also to adults. This instinct is one of the most important sources of all societal evolution. In maternal love we find the source of love in general. It is not identical in quality with sexual love, which is related rather to the egoistic instinct of hunger. Sexuality has more in common with cruelty than it does with love, but when combined with love, it is a highly refined product of cultural evolution. In the case of primitive peoples sexuality is relatively seldom associated with "love," whereas an asexual emotion of maternal tenderness, even between adults, is found quite frequently.

By regarding a man's love as the product of his feminine-maternal instincts, Briffault assumes a bisexual tendency in every individual. According to him, it is not only love and tenderness that have their origin in maternal love but compassion, generosity, and benevolence as well—in short, all "altruistic" feelings, even in their most abstract and general manifestations. The child's love for the mother originates in the need for protection and help; the herd instinct derives from the child's fear and defenselessness. Similarly, the primitive's hostility toward the stranger is not something innate nor does it express a "natural" aggressive drive but is the product of the actual circumstances in the life of primitive groups that inevitably lead to mutual distrust.

Briffault bases an ingenious theory about the difference between the animal herd and the animal family on the contrast between the sex drive and maternal love. In his view, the herd is the exclusive product of male sexual impulses and lacks stability, whereas the family arises as a result of the influence of maternal instincts and forms the core of all lasting social groupings. The primitive human group does not evolve from the animal herd but from the animal family. The merging of these families, which are formed by the bonding of the mother with her offspring and bear no resemblance to the later patriarchal family, inevitably leads to the establishment of a primitive society centered around the mother.

Exogamy and the incest taboo are not the result of innate instinct nor of a natural selection countering the harmful effects of incest. In novel fashion, which I can't go into here, Briffault attempts to explain exogamy from the structure of matricentric society. In the course of his exposition he indicates the extent to which a last trace of the original matriarchal familial order, the matrilocal marriage, still exists worldwide: the husband frequently moves into the wife's house, and in the matter of the line of descent, the mother's family is usually the determining factor. In the transition to patrilocal marriage brought about by the introduction of private property, the consent of the bride's family is purchased by a gift or a service performed by the bridegroom.

In most primitive societies women have an extraordinarily high degree of independence, which is based on the fact of the division of labor and the associated economic functions assigned to females. It is a mistake to conclude that because the woman works hard she occupies a low position in society. The matriarchal (gynecocratic) structure must be clearly distinguished from the matricentric structure, that is, a societal order characterized by the relatively great social and psychic influence of the woman. In a gynecocratic structure the woman rules over the man. Every relationship involving domination depends on the presence of private property and its defense. Matriarchy in this narrower sense can therefore be found only in relatively highly developed societies.

Marriage has an essentially economic function and is by no means a "natural" arrangement. Thus, it is not linked, not even in its origins, to claims to the exclusive sexual possession of the partner. Just as there is not—to begin with—a "natural" monogamous instinct, neither is there jealousy based on a need for exclusive possession of the sexual object. In the case of primitive man, jealousy doesn't have to do with his concern to preserve the exclusivity of his rights but is associated with fear of not being supplied with sexual objects. In other words, he fears that his wife will be abducted, not that she will be seduced. Because sexuality is less repressed in primitive society, it lacks the sentiments of romantic love but also the emotional deformities or pathological manifestations resulting from sexual repression. The proclivity to be monogamous is not the cause but the result of the institution of monogamous marriage. Its evolution is influenced primarily by economic and social changes in society. The turning point is the transition to ownership of herds, which gives the husband increased purchasing power and with it economic superiority over the wife. When this herdsman stage is lacking, the original matricentric conditions endure longer. Whereas marriage from primitive to Roman times served a primarily economic and not a sexual function, the institution of Christian marriage has the tendency to unite both aspects and thus to give love and sexuality, as well as economic interests, their due.

Briffault treats the evolution of religion and morality in

great detail. I shall cite only a few examples from the wealth of his material:

• Taboo, which he sees as the model for all irrational morality, is traced back to the prohibition against sexual intercourse during menstruation that the woman imposes on the man.

• He suggests that the rise of totemism is due to the fact that the most important food originally shared by a tribe takes on a sacred character.

• He regards the rise of a sense of individuality as a consequence of the introduction of the concept of private property. It is not instincts of individuality that create private property; the latter produces what are mistakenly believed to be natural instincts.

• In his discussion of the role of the moon in primitive cosmology he notes that the waning and waxing of the moon are closely connected to the thoughts and desires primitive people have concerning death and resurrection. It is not until agriculture is introduced that the sun plays an ever greater role.

• Primitive religious ideas definitely do not spring from a "worship of nature" but from the desire to attain magical powers.

Woman plays a major and usually underestimated role in the evolution of religion. The great goddesses, who occupied an important position in Near Eastern and European cultures, owed their role essentially to their connection with agricultural rites and to that magical gift of natural productiveness attributed specifically to woman. The high point of religious evolution is attained when the goddess is no longer feared and worshiped as the possessor of magical powers but is celebrated as the virgin mother of the divine child. Religious feeling is associated here for the first time with love; the transition from timeworn national tribal deities to gentle world deities occurred first in the figure of the Great Mother. As primitive magic gradually becomes transformed into a "theological" religion as a result of the workings of the male intellect, the woman loses her prominent position in religion.

The evolution of morality is strongly influenced by morality's origins in taboo. Primitive taboos as the source of sexual morality, as well as of morality in general, are strengthened by the male desire for property, which is what gives the gradual development of this morality its impetus. It is by no means female "nature" that has required extreme chastity, nor is it female jealousy that has enforced monogamy. Quite the contrary: matriarchal societies are characterized by a high degree of sexual freedom and laxity. Whereas the original primitive taboos and the moral feelings associated with them are of a ubiquitous nature, that form of sexual morality which demands chastity arises along with the evolution of patriarchal society and the economic conditions underlying it. Chastity was first a ritual requirement for attaining magical powers—as in the Near East, Egypt, and Greece—and a civic virtue—as in Rome. It was not until the advent of Christianity that chastity attained the status of a high ethical or religious value. Even though a variety of views concerning the degree of sinfulness of sexual intercourse arose in the history of Christian thought, there was never any doubt that virginity was superior to marriage. The beliefs of the Church Fathers presented the strongest possible contrast to the ideas and customs of the European barbarians with whom they came in contact. The gradual change that Christian rigor brought about in sexual attitudes expressed itself first in literature and then gradually, albeit never completely, in social life.

Briffault's book has been reviewed widely, especially in England and America (Cf. Ellis 1928; Ludivici 1927; Malinowski

1927; Ayres 1927; Langdon-Davies 1927; Ginsberg 1927; Goldenweiser 1928). The reviews, some of them quite detailed, alternate between enthusiastic approval and—especially those by ethnologists—cool rejection.

The ethnological layman is certainly not equipped to decide in the case of this or that specific point whether Briffault's arguments or those of his opponents have more validity. But as I indicated initially, his book reaches far beyond the framework of individual ethnological issues; by virtue of the unusual breadth of the material and the author's rare intellectual independence and originality, this work represents an important contribution to the field of social psychology. As for the subject of Mother Right, Briffault takes it up at the point where L. H. Morgan had left off.

Using the method of historical materialism, he attempts to explain changes in sentiments and institutions on the basis of changes in everyday life, specifically in economic conditions. I believe the major significance of this unusual book lies both in its recognition of the social determination of all sentiments, even those that appear to be the most natural, and in its attempt to make use of extensive empirical material to explain their development on the basis of specific societal changes.

Within the scope of this discussion, my critical remarks can address only general matters and not specific questions. In his Preface Briffault himself anticipates an important consideration when he points to the unfavorable external conditions under which the book was written. Thus, portions of it are unevenly developed, both quantitatively and qualitatively. Even more important is the reverse side of his intellectual autonomy and independence: he does not consider the earlier or contemporary authors whose research took the same direction as his, or if he does, then only minimally. For example, he reexamines completely *ab ovo* questions that had already been treated extensively in the French Enlightenment, such as the social determination of sentiments; furthermore, he does not mention Marx and Engels at all; and finally, he takes scarcely any notice of the recent literature in ethnopsychology. This is particularly noticeable in his examination of the question of the apparently altruistic character of the primitive mother's love. In this connection, the fact that he does not adequately take into account the Durkheim school's studies of primitive society, and in particular Lévy-Brühl's works on the primitive mind, represents a serious flaw.

I cannot refrain from making a critical observation concerning one other point. In his summarizing last chapter, Briffault speaks of woman's "innate conservatism" and states that in a wider sense every woman stops learning after the age of twenty-five. Because he took such great pains to establish so convincingly that sentiments are socially determined and displayed in this regard a decided advance over the views of the Romantics and also of Bachofen, a "slip" like this is all the more surprising. It shows, of course, how deeply rooted in the unconscious, even of an author as progressive as Briffault, are traditional, biologically based value judgments. Taken in its totality, however, his work leaves even critical readers with a great many stimulating ideas and a great deal of information as well as with the impression of a significant scholarly achievement.

*—Translated by Hunter Hannum*
*and Hildegarde Hannum*

# 5

## The Significance of the Theory of Mother Right for Today (1970)

The fact that Bachofen's theories of Mother Right and the matriarchal societies found relatively little attention in the nineteenth century and the first half of the twentieth is sufficiently explained by the circumstance that up to the end of the First World War the patriarchal system in Europe and America had remained unshaken, so that the very idea of women as the center of a social and religious structure seemed unthinkable and absurd. By the same token, the social and psychological changes that have taken place in the last four decades should provide the reason the problem of matriarchate should arouse new and intense interest; only now, it seems, are changes occurring which call for a new evaluation of ideas that had remained dormant for more than a hundred years. Before writing about these changes, however, let me give the reader not familiar with Bachofen and Morgan a brief introduction to their view of the principles and values of matriarchal society.

According to Bachofen, the matriarchal principle is that of

life, unity, and peace. The woman, in caring for the infant, extends her love beyond her own self to other human beings, and projects all her gifts and imagination to the aim of preserving and beautifying the existence of another human being. The principle of matriarchy is that of universality, while the patriarchal system is that of restrictions. The idea of the universal brotherhood of man is rooted in the principle of motherhood, but vanishes with the development of patriarchal society. Matriarchate is the basis of the principle of universal freedom and equality, of peace and tender humaneness. It is also the basis for principled concern for material welfare and worldly happiness. (Bachofen 1967, 69–121)

Quite independently, L. H. Morgan came to the conclusion (tentatively, in his *Systems of Consanguinity and Affinity*, 1870, and more definitely in *Ancient Society*, 1877) that the kingship system of the American Indians—similar to that found in Asia, Africa, and Australia, was based on the matriarchal principle, and he asserted that the higher forms of civilization "will be a repetition, but on a higher level of the principles of liberty, equality and fraternity which characterized the ancient gens." Even this brief presentation of these principles of matriarchate should make clear why I attach such importance to the following social-psychological changes:

1. The failure of the patriarchal-authoritarian system to fulfill its function; its inability to prevent large and devastating wars and terroristic dictatorships; its incapacity to act in order to prevent future catastrophes, such as nuclear-biological-chemical war, starvation in large parts of the colonial world, and the catastrophic results of increasing poisoning of air, water, and soil.

2. The democratic revolution, which has defeated the traditional authoritarian structures and replaced them with democratic structures. The process of democratization has gone

together with the emergence of a technological, affluent society that does not mainly require personal obedience but operates, rather, on the basis of teamwork and manipulated consent.

3. The women's revolution, which, although not complete, has gone a long way in carrying out the radical ideas of the Enlightenment about the equality of men and women. This revolution has dealt a severe blow to patriarchal authority in the capitalist countries as well as in a country as conservative as the Soviet Union.

4. The children's and adolescents' revolution: In the past, children were able to rebel only in inadequate ways—refusing to eat, crying, constipation, bed wetting, and general obstinacy, but since the nineteenth century they have found spokesmen (Pestalozzi, Freud, and others) who stressed that children have a will and passions of their own and must be taken seriously. This trend continued with increasing force and insight in the twentieth century, and Dr. Benjamin Spock became its most influential spokesman. As far as adolescents and post-adolescents are concerned, they now speak for themselves—and no longer in a subdued voice. They demand the right to be heard, to be taken seriously, to be active subjects and not passive objects in the arrangement governing their lives. They attack patriarchal authority directly, vigorously—and sometimes viciously.

5. The vision of the consumer's paradise. Our consumer culture creates a new vision: If we continue on the path of technological progress, we shall eventually arrive at a point where no desire, not even the ever newly created ones, remains unfulfilled; fulfillment will be instant and without the need to exert any effort. In this vision, technique assumes the characteristics of the Great Mother, a technical instead of a natural one, who nurses her children and pacifies them with a never ceasing lullaby (in the form of radio and television). In the process, man becomes emotionally an infant, feeling secure in

the hope that mother's breasts will always supply abundant milk and that decisions need no longer be made by the individual. Instead, they are made by the technological apparatus itself, interpreted and executed by the technocrats, the new priests of an emerging matriarchal religion, with Technique as its goddess.

6. Certain matriarchal tendencies can also be observed in some sectors of the—more or less—radical youth. Not only because they are strictly antiauthoritarian, but also because of their embracing of the above-mentioned values and attitudes of the matriarchal world, as described by Bachofen and Morgan. The idea of group sex (whether in its middle class, suburban forms or in radical communes with shared sex) has a close connection with Bachofen's description of the early matriarchal stage of mankind. The question can also be raised as to whether the tendency to diminish sexual differences in appearance, dress, etc., is not also related to the tendency to abolish the traditional status of the male, and to make the two sexes less polarized, leading to regression (emotionally) to the pregenital stage of the infant.

There are other traits which tend to support the assumption that there is an increasing matriarchal trend among this section of the young generation. The "group" itself seems to assume the function of the mother; the need for immediate satisfaction of desires, the passive-receptive attitude which is most clearly indicated in the drug obsession, the need to huddle together and to touch each other physically—all seem to indicate a regression to the infant's tie to mother. In all these respects the young generation does not seem to be as different from their elders as they think themselves to be, although their consumption patterns have a different content and their despair is expressed overtly and aggressively. The disturbing element in this neomatriarchalism is that it is a mere negation of patriarchalism and a straight regression to an infantile pattern, rather than a dialectical progression to a higher form of matriarchalism. H. Marcuse's appeal to the young seems to rest largely on the fact that he is the spokesman for infantile regression to matriarchalism and that he makes this principle more attractive by using revolutionary rhetoric.

7. Perhaps not unrelated to these social changes is a development in psychoanalysis that is beginning to correct Freud's older idea about the central role of the sexual bond between son and mother, and the resulting hostility toward the father, with the new notion that there is an early "preoedipal" intense bond between the infant and the mother, regardless of the child's sex. Bachofen's work, if thoroughly studied by psychoanalysts, will prove to be of immense value for the understanding of this nonsexual mother fixation.

I want to conclude these introductory remarks with a theoretical consideration. The matriarchal principle is that of unconditional love, natural equality, emphasis on the bonds of blood and soil, compassion and mercy; the patriarchal principle is that of conditional love, hierarchical structure, abstract thought, man-made laws, the state and justice. In the last analysis, mercy and justice represent the two principles, respectively.

It seems that in the course of history the two principles have sometimes clashed with each other violently and that sometimes they formed a synthesis (for instance in the Catholic Church, or in Marx's concept of socialism). If they are opposed to each other, the matriarchal principle manifests itself in motherly overindulgence and infantilization of the child, preventing its full maturity; fatherly authority becomes harsh domination and control, based on the child's fear and feelings of guilt. This is the case in the relationship of the child to father-mother, as well as in the spirit of patriarchal and matriarchal societies which determine the family structure. The purely matriarchal society stands in the way of the full development of the individual, thus preventing technical, rational, artistic progress. The purely patriarchal society cares nothing for love and equality; it is only concerned with man-made laws, the state, abstract principles, obedience. It is beautifully described in Sophocles' *Antigone* in the person and system of Creon, the prototype of a fascist leader. (Cf. the discussion of this point in Fromm 1951a, chapter 5.)

When the patriarchal and matriarchal principles form a synthesis, however, each of the two principles is colored by the other: motherly love by justice and rationality, and fatherly love by mercy and equality.

Today the fight against patriarchal authority seems to be destroying the patriarchal principle, suggesting a return to a matriarchal principle in a regressive and nondialectic way. A viable and progressive solution lies only in a new synthesis of the opposites, one in which the opposition between mercy and justice is replaced by a union of the two on a higher level.

# II

Sex Differences and Character

# ·6

## Sex and Character (1943)

The thesis that between the two sexes there are innate differences which necessarily result in basic differences in character and fate is a very old one. The Old Testament makes it woman's peculiarity and curse that her "desire shall be to thy husband and he shall rule over thee" and man's that he shall have to work in sweat and sorrow. But even the biblical report contains virtually the opposite thesis: man was created in God's likeness, and only as punishment for man's and woman's original disobedience—they were treated as equals with regard to their moral responsibility—were they cursed with mutual conflict and eternal difference. Both these views, that of their basic difference and that of their basic identity, have been repeated through the centuries—one age or one philosophical school emphasizing the one, another the opposite, thesis.

The problem assumed increased significance in the philosophical and political discussions of the eighteenth and nineteenth centuries. Representatives of the Enlightenment philosophy took the position that there were no innate differences between the sexes (*l'âme n'a pas de sexe*); that whatever differences could be observed were conditioned by difference in education, were—as would be said today—cultural differences. Romantic philosophers of the early nineteenth century, on the other hand, stressed the very opposite point. They analyzed the characterological differences between men and women and said that the fundamental differences were the result of innate biological and physiological differences. Their contention was that these differences in character would exist in any conceivable culture.

Regardless of the merits of the respective arguments—and the analysis of the Romantics was often profound—they both had a political implication. The enlightened philosophers, especially the French, wanted to make a point for the social— and to some extent political—equality of men and women. They emphasized the lack of innate differences as an argument for their case. The Romantics, who were political reactionaries, used their analysis of the essence—*Wesen*—of woman's nature as a proof for the necessity of political and social inequality. Although they attributed very admirable qualities to "the woman," they insisted that her characteristics made her unfit to participate in social and political life on an equal footing with men.

The political struggle for woman's equality did not end in the nineteenth century, nor did the theoretical discussion on the innate versus the cultural character of their differences. In modern psychology Freud became the most outspoken representative of the Romantics' cause. Whereas their argument had been couched in philosophical language, his was based on the scientific observation of patients in the psychoanalytic procedure. He assumed that the anatomical difference between the sexes was the cause for unalterable characterological differences. "Anatomy is her fate," he says of the woman, paraphrasing a sentence of Napoleon's. His contention was that the little girl, when she discovers the fact that she lacks the male genital organ, is profoundly shocked and impressed by this discovery; that she feels something she ought to have is lacking; that she envies men for having what fate has denied her; that in the normal course of development she will try to overcome her feeling of inferiority and envy by substituting other things for the male genital organ: children, husband, or possessions. In the case of neurotic development she does not succeed in making such satisfactory substitutions. She remains envious of all men, does not give up her wish to be a man herself, becomes homosexual or hates men, or seeks certain culturally permitted compensations. Even in the case of normal development, the tragic quality of woman's fate never quite disappears; she is cursed with a wish to obtain something which remains unattainable throughout her life.

Although orthodox psychoanalysts retained this theory of Freud as one of the cornerstones of their psychological system, another group of culturally oriented psychoanalysts disputed Freud's findings. They showed the fallacies—clinically and theoretically—in Freud's reasoning by pointing to the cultural and personal experiences of women in modern society which caused the characterological results which he had explained on biological grounds. The views of this group of psychoanalysts found confirmation in the findings of the anthropologists.

Nevertheless, there exists a certain danger that some followers of those progressive anthropological and psychoanalytic theories will lean over backwards and deny completely that biological differences have any effect in molding the character structure. They may be prompted to do so by the same motivation which was found in the representatives of the French Enlightenment. Since the emphasis on innate differences is used as an argument by the enemies of woman's equality, it may seem necessary to prove that there were none but cultural causes for any differences which may be empirically observed.

It is important to recognize that a significant philosophical question is involved in this whole controversy. The tendency to deny any characterological differences between the sexes may be prompted by the implicit acceptance of one of the premises of antiequalitarian philosophy: in order to demand equality one has to prove that there are no characterological differences between the sexes except those caused directly by existing social conditions. The whole discussion is particularly involved because one group is speaking of differences whereas the reactionaries really mean deficiencies—and more specifically those deficiencies which make it impossible for full equality to be shared with the majority group. Thus women's limited intelligence and lack of faculties for organization and for abstraction or critical judgment were held to preclude their full equality with men. One school of thought said they possessed intuition, love, and so on but that these qualities did not seem to make them more fit for the task of modern society. The same is often said about minorities such as the Negroes or the Jews. Thus the psychologist or anthropologist was put in a position where he had to disprove that among sex or racial groups, there were any fundamental differences which had anything to do with their ability to share full equality. In this position, the liberal thinker was inclined to minimize the existence of any distinctions.

Though the liberals proved that differences justifying political, economic, and social inequality do not exist, they allowed themselves to be pushed into a strategically unfavorable defensive position. Establishing the fact that there are no socially damaging differences does not require one to hold there are no differences at all. Properly then, the question is: What use is made of the existing or alleged differences, and what political purposes do they serve? Even granted that women show certain characterological differences from men, what does it mean?

It is the thesis of this paper that certain biological differences result in characterological differences; that such differences are blended with those which are directly produced by social factors; that the latter are much stronger in their effect and can either increase, eliminate, or reverse biologically rooted differences; and that eventually characterological differences between the sexes, inasmuch as they are not directly determined by culture, never constitute differences in value. In other words, characterological differences are differences not in terms of "good" or "bad" but only in terms of coloring—the kind of virtues and vices peculiar to any large group. To be more specific, the character typical of men and women in Western culture is determined by their respective social roles, but there is a coloring of character which is rooted in sex differences. This coloring is insignificant in comparison with the socially rooted differences, but it must not be entirely neglected.

The implicit assumption underlying much reactionary thinking is that equality presupposes an absence of differences between persons or social groups. Since obviously such differences exist with regard to practically everything that matters in life, their conclusion is that there can be no equality. When, conversely, the liberals are moved to deny the fact that there are great differences in mental and physical gifts and favorable or unfavorable accidental personality conditions, they only help their adversaries to appear right in the eyes of the common man. The concept of equality as it has developed in Judaeo-Christian and in modern progressive traditions means that all men are equal in such basic human capacities as those making for the enjoyment of freedom and happiness. It means, furthermore, that as a political consequence of this basic equality no man shall be made the means to the ends of another man, no group the means to the ends of another group. Each man is a universe for himself and is only his own purpose. His goal is the realization of his being, including those very peculiarities which are characteristic of him and make him different from others. Thus equality is the basis for the full development of differences, and it results in the development of individuality.

Although there are a number of biological differences which might well be examined with regard to their relevance to character differences between men and women, this paper will deal mainly with only one. Our purpose here is not so much to examine the whole problem of character differences between the sexes as to illustrate the general thesis. We shall mainly concern ourselves with the respective roles of men and women in sexual intercourse and shall undertake to show that this difference results in certain characterological differences—differences that only color the main differences that arise from the difference in their social roles.

In order to function sexually, the man must have an erection and must be able to retain it during intercourse until he has had an orgasm; in order to satisfy the woman, he must be able to retain the erection for a sufficiently long time so that she may have an orgasm. This means that in order to satisfy the woman sexually the man has to demonstrate that he has the ability to have and maintain an erection. The woman, on the other hand, in order to satisfy the man sexually needs demonstrate nothing. To be sure, her excitement may enhance the man's pleasure. Certain accompanying physical changes in her sexual organs may make intercourse easier for him. Since only purely sexual reactions are to be considered—not the subtle, psychic reactions of differentiated personalities—the fact remains that the man needs to have an erection to satisfy the woman, the woman needs to have nothing but a certain amount of willingness to satisfy the man. In speaking of willingness it is important to note that the woman's availability for the sexual satisfaction of the man is dependent on her will; it is a conscious decision she can make at any time she pleases.

The man's availability, however, is by no means simply a function of his will. As a matter of fact, he may have sexual desire and an erection against his will, and he may be impotent despite an ardent wish to the contrary. Furthermore, on the man's side an inability to function is a fact which cannot be concealed. The woman's lack of either total or partial response, her "failure," although often recognizable to the man, is by no means similarly obvious; it permits a great deal of deception. If the woman consents with her will, the man can be sure of being satisfied whenever he desires her. But the situation of the woman is entirely different; the most ardent sexual desire on her side will not lead to satisfaction unless the man is sufficiently desirous of her to have an erection. And even during the sexual act the woman must depend for her full satisfaction on the man's ability to carry her to orgasm. Thus, to satisfy the partner, the man has to prove something; the woman does not.

From this difference in their respective sexual roles something else follows—the difference in their specific anxieties connected with the sexual function. The anxiety is located at the very spot where the man and woman's position is vulnerable. The man's position is vulnerable insofar as he has to prove something, that is, insofar as he can potentially fail. To him intercourse has always the coloring of a test, of an examination. His specific anxiety is that of failing. Fear of castration is the extreme case—fear of becoming organically and therefore permanently unable to perform. The woman's vulnerability, on the other hand, lies in her dependency on the man; the element of insecurity connected with her sexual function lies not in failing but in being "left alone," in being frustrated, in not having complete control over the process which leads to sexual satisfaction. It is not surprising, then, that the anxieties of men and women refer to different spheres—the man's concerning his ego, his prestige, his value in the eyes of the woman; the woman's concerning her sexual pleasure and satisfaction.

The reader may now ask: Are not these anxieties characteristic only of neurotic personalities? Is not the normal man sure of his potency? Is not the normal woman sure of her partner? Is one not concerned here with the highly nervous and sexually insecure modern man? Are not the "cave man" and the "cave woman" with their "primitive" and unspoiled sexuality free from such doubts and anxieties?

At first glance, this might seem to be the case. The man who is constantly worried about his potency is characteristic of a certain type of neurotic personality, as is the woman who is constantly afraid of remaining unsatisfied or who suffers from her dependency. Here—as is so often the case—the difference between the "neurotic" and the "normal" is more one of degree and of awareness than one of essential quality. What appears as a conscious and continuous anxiety in the neurotic person is relatively unnoticed and quantitatively slight anxiety in the so-called normal man. The same is true in the case of women. Furthermore, in normal individuals anxieties are not aroused by certain incidents which are sure to cause manifest anxiety in the neurotic person. The normal man does not doubt his potency. The normal woman is not afraid of being sexually frustrated by the man she has chosen for a sexual partner. To choose the very man whom she can have "faith" in sexually is an essential part of her healthy sexual instinct. This in no way alters the fact that potentially the man can fail—but never the woman. The woman is dependent on the man's desire, not the man on hers.

Since it is important that this point be clear, let us illustrate further with a parallel from another field. Consider the difference between an actor or a speaker and a person in his audience. Though an actor or speaker is anxious each time he has to perform—and experienced persons can worry about failing, for some anxiety seems to be present with most people who have to perform—there are certainly others who do not feel any anxiety. Nevertheless, the fact that even the latter find that a successful performance brings a kind of relief which results in elation or happiness suggests that they were not wholly unaware of the possibility of failing.

There is still another element which is significant in determining the presence of anxieties and of different anxieties in the normal man and woman.

The difference between the sexes is the basis for the earliest and most elementary division of mankind into separate groups. Man and woman need each other; biologically, for the maintenance of the race and of the family; psychologically, for the satisfaction of their sexual desires. But in any situation in which two different groups need each other there will be elements not only of harmony, cooperation, and mutual satisfaction, but also of struggle and disharmony.

Love and antagonism are two sides of a basic constellation—difference with interdependence. The sexual relationship between the sexes could scarcely be free from potential antagonism and hostility. Men and women have, along with the capacity to love each other, a similar capacity to hate. In any man–woman relationship the element of antagonism is a potentiality, and from this very potentiality the element of anxiety as well must at times arise. The beloved one may turn into an enemy, and then the vulnerable points of man and woman respectively are threatened.

This concept of male–female anxiety is significantly different from that of Freud. The author follows Freud in assuming potential antagonism between the sexes; the difference lies in the nature of this antagonism. Freud's basic attitude is patriarchal; therefore, the main conflict which exists is the one between father and son. The woman is not important enough to threaten as does the father. The main fear in man, to Freud, is the fear of castration. This fear, however, is primarily a threat arising not from the woman but from the father who is jealous of the incestuous wishes of the son. Only secondarily is the man's castration fear directed toward woman. Since woman to him is only a sexually inferior and not a sexually different being, he cannot perceive that man is as much afraid of woman as he is of the father.

It should also be noted in passing that anxiety concerning the sexual organs differs in men and women. In the male the extreme form of such anxiety carries the idea that his sexual organ will be cut off. With some exceptions woman's anxiety about her genitals does not refer to anything being cut off or having been cut off. She fears the injury of the inner part of her body. The vagina is an entrance into the body—as well as a delicate and very important organ of the female body. There is reason to assume that in everyone there exists a potential anxiety about injury through the openings into the body. But, although other openings may be more or less adequately protected, this is by no means so clearly the case with the vagina— as first parental strictness and then rumors and fantasies of criminal assault have tended to impress upon the child. Woman's normal anxiety is not castration but defenselessness toward an internal injury—such as the incurring of pregnancy against her will.

In describing the difference in kind of the anxiety specific for men and women respectively, we have already discussed one characterological difference resulting from the difference in the sexual roles. The specific kind of anxiety results in specific trends to overcome it.

If the man's main anxiety is that of failing in or not performing the expected task, the drive designed to protect him from this anxiety is the wish for prestige. The man is deeply pervaded by a craving to prove constantly to himself, to the woman he loves, to all other women, and to all other men that he lives up to any expectation of him. He seeks reassurance against the fear of sexual failing by competing in all other spheres of life in which will power, physical strength, and intelligence are useful in assuring success. Closely linked with this craving for prestige is his competitive attitude toward other men. Being afraid of possible failure, he tends to prove that he is better than any other man. The Don Juan does so directly in the sexual realm, the average man indirectly—by killing more enemies, hunting more deer, making more money, or being more successful in other ways than his male competitors.

It must be realized that the particular sexual role of the man is but a minor source of the craving for prestige and competitiveness in comparison with cravings of a social and cultural nature. As a number of psychoanalytic, anthropological, and sociological writers have indicated, such cravings chiefly result from the kind of experiences both the child and the adult have in any given culture. It has been shown that when anxiety is aroused in the child he feels powerless and inferior; it is therefore imperative for him to find recognition by others, to be popular, and to be superior to competitors. The modern social and economic system is based on the principles of competition and success; ideologies praise its value, and by these and other circumstances the craving for prestige and competitiveness are firmly implanted in the average human being living in the Western culture. Even if there were no difference in the respective sexual roles, these cravings would exist in men and women on the strength of social factors. The impact of these social sources is so great that it might seem doubtful whether—in quantitative terms—there is any marked predominance of the craving for prestige in men as a result of the sexual factors which this chapter discusses. The matter of first importance is not quantity or degree to which competitiveness is increased by the sexual sources but rather the need that recognition be given to the presence of any factor other than the socially conditioned ones which make for competitiveness. It happens that in Western culture the cultural pressure with men moves in the same direction as the sexual factors. With women, also, the cultural and sexual factors used to operate in the same direction; but with the fundamental change in woman's position, which drew her increasingly into the same social and economic conditions that determine man's life, the social factors have become the same for men and women, and there is even now sufficient empirical evidence to recognize that these social factors prove to be stronger than the sexual ones.

The masculine striving for prestige throws some light on the specific quality of male vanity. It is generally said that women are vainer than men. Although the reverse may be true, what matters is not the difference in quantity but in the nature of the vanity. The essential feature of man's vanity is to show off, to demonstrate what a good "performer" he is. He acts as if he lived in an unending examination dream. He is eager to assert that he is not afraid of failing. This vanity seems to color all of man's activity. There is probably no achievement of men, from making love to the most courageous acts in fighting or thinking, which is not colored to some degree by this typical male vanity; insofar as this is the case, his activity is lacking in seriousness.

Another aspect of man's craving for prestige is his sensitivity toward ridicule, and particularly toward ridicule from women. Even a coward may become something of a hero under the fear of being ridiculed by women, and the fear of losing one's life may be less than the fear of ridicule. As a matter of fact, this is typical in the pattern of male heroism, which is no greater than the heroism of which women are capable but different because it is colored by the male sort of vanity.

Another result of man's precarious position toward woman and his fear of her ridicule is his hatred for her. This hatred contributes to a striving which has also a defensive function: to dominate the woman, to have power over her, to make her feel weak and inferior. If he succeeds in this, he need not be afraid of her. If she is afraid of him—afraid of being killed, beaten, or starved—she cannot ridicule him. Power over a person is dependent neither on one's intensity of passion nor on the functioning of one's sexual and emotional productiveness. Power depends on factors which can be so securely maintained that no doubt of incompetency need ever arise. Incidentally, the promise of power over woman is the comfort which the patriarchally biased biblical myth holds out to the man even while God curses him.

One last trait, in man, should be mentioned—one that results from his fear of failure, not so much because it is a "normal" trait but because it links with a problem which psychoanalytic literature has dealt with: the man's wish to be a woman. Though Freud quite naturally assumed that a general feature of woman's psychology is her wish to be a man, other psychoanalytic thinkers have recognized in men the presence of wishes to be a woman and have offered various explanations. To one of these explanations—man's envy of the woman's capacity to bear children—reference will be made presently. The aim here is to point to the connection between man's need to prove something and his wish to be a woman. His "test" situation is a continuous burden. He would be greatly relieved if he could escape his burden—and he could, if he were a woman. In the normal man, however, the wish is scarcely conscious and, in quantity, very small. In the neurotic man the wish to be a woman can be extremely strong, whether it is entertained consciously or repressed. Its strength depends on the intensity of the fear of failure in performance, which in turn is rooted in the whole personality structure.

Just as certain characterological trends spring from the main anxiety of men—failure—others spring from the main fear of women—frustration and dependency. The fear of being left alone—in the sexual act itself as well as emotionally and socially—and the fear of being dependent comprise a trait which is generally supposed to be typically feminine. This dependency is traced back to woman's "nature." The traditional role of women in any patriarchal culture is such that the fear of dependency is aroused regardless of any conditions specific to her sex role; but, again, social conditions are mistaken for natural ones. Despite the conventional fallacy about woman's nature, however, in the statement about woman's dependency there is a kernel of truth which should not be neglected. This is the result of her specific sexual role which will now be recapitulated. The woman does not need to prove anything. She need not be afraid of failure, but in her sexual satisfaction she is dependent on something outside herself—the man's desire for her and his potency to carry through this desire. He is never entirely sure whether he will succeed, and this fear hurts his pride. She is never entirely sure whether she can rely on him, and this fear makes her feel insecure and anxious in a different way.

One trait resulting from this position of the woman is vanity, but a vanity different in nature from the man's. His vanity is to show what he can do, to prove that he never fails; her vanity is essentially a need to attract, and the need to prove to herself that she can attract, is attractive. To be sure, the man needs to attract a woman sexually in order to win her. This holds true especially in a culture where differentiated tastes and feelings are involved in sexual attraction. But there are other ways by which he can gain her and induce her to be his sexual partner: sheer physical power or, more significantly, social power and wealth. His opportunities for sexual satisfaction do not depend solely on his sexual attractiveness. Her sexual satisfaction depends entirely on her attractiveness. Neither force nor promises can make a man sexually potent. The woman's attempt to be attractive is necessitated by her sexual role, and her vanity or concern with her attractiveness results from this.

The woman's fear of dependency, of frustration, of a role which forces her to wait, frequently leads to a wish which Freud has stressed heavily: the wish to have the male genital organ. The root for this wish, however, is not that the woman primarily feels she lacks something, that she is inferior to the man for want of the penis. Although in many instances there are other reasons, the wish of the woman to have a penis often springs from her wish not to be dependent, not to be restricted in her activity, not to be exposed to the danger of frustration. Just as the man's wish to be a woman may result from his desire to be rid of the burden of the test, the woman's wish to have a penis may result from her desire to overcome her dependence. Also, under special circumstances, but not infrequently, not only does the penis serve as a symbol of independence but, in the service of sadistic-aggressive tendencies, it also symbolizes a weapon with which to hurt men or other women.

If the man's main weapon against the woman is his physical and social power over her, then her main weapon is her ability to ridicule him. The most radical way in which to ridicule him is to make him impotent. There are many ways, including crude and subtle ones, for the woman to do this. They range from the expressed or implied expectation of his failure to frigidity and the sort of vaginal spasm which makes intercourse physically impossible. The wish to castrate the man does not seem to play the all-important role which Freud ascribes to it.

To be sure, one way is to express a wish to render the man impotent, and this often appears unquestionably when destructive and sadistic tendencies are marked. But the main aim of woman's hostility does not seem to be physical but functional damage—to interfere with the man's ability to perform. Man's specific hostility is to overpower; woman's to undermine.

There are other sexual differences which may have a bearing on characterological differences between men and women. The woman's genital organs are more differentiated than the man's, for she has two sources of excitement. The main source of the woman's excitement happens to be within her body, the man's on the outside. In the man something easily visible happens when he is sexually excited; in the woman this is not the case. The sexual act for the woman implies the possibility of pregnancy, with the ensuing profound change in her glandular processes, but no such profound change in the man's organism is connected with his sexual activity. It is not our intention to take up these problems in this chapter, but there is one more difference which may well be discussed because it has been somewhat neglected in the classic psychoanalytic literature.

Women can bear children; man cannot. Characteristically, from his patriarchal viewpoint, Freud assumed that the woman is envious of the male organ, but he scarcely noted the possibility that men are envious of women's ability to bear children. This one-sided view not only comes from the masculine premise that men are superior to women but also results from the attitude of a highly technical-industrial civilization in which natural productiveness is not very highly valued. Nevertheless, if one considers earlier periods of human history, when life depended essentially on the productivity of nature and not on technical productivity, the fact that women shared this gift with the soil and with female animals must have been exceedingly impressive. Man is sterile—if only the purely naturalistic realm is considered. In a culture in which the main emphasis was on natural productivity, one would assume that the man felt inferior to the woman, especially when his role in the production of the child was not clearly understood. It is safe to assume that man admired woman for this capacity which he lacked, that he was awed by her and envious of her. He could not produce; he could only kill animals so that he could eat them, or kill enemies so that he could be safe or acquire their strength in some magical way.

Without discussing the place of these influences in more purely agrarian communities, we shall touch briefly on the effects of some important historical changes. One of the most significant of these was the increasing application of the technical mode of production. More and more the mind was used to improve and increase the various means of living that originally were dependent on nature's gifts alone. Although women originally had a gift that made them superior to men and the latter originally compensated for, this lack by using their skill for destruction, men later came to use their reason as the basis for rational productivity. In its earlier stages this was closely linked with magic; in its present highly developed stage, with science. Women are physiologically equipped to produce; men prove their productivity by determined rational effort.

Rather than develop this topic at this point, we shall merely refer to the writings of Bachofen, Morgan, and Briffault, who have gathered and brilliantly analyzed anthropological material which, though it may not prove their theses, strongly suggests that in several phases of early history certain cultures existed in which social organization was centered around the mother and in which mother-goddesses, identified with the productivity of nature, were the center of man's religious ideas.

One illustration will suffice. The Babylonian myth of creation starts with the existence of a mother-goddess—Tiamat—who rules over the universe. Her rule, however, is threatened by her male sons, who are planning to rebel and overthrow her. They seek as a leader for this fight—somebody who can match her strength. Eventually they agree on Marduk but, before definitely choosing him, require him to undergo a test. What is the test? A coat is brought to him. He must "with the power of his mouth" make the coat disappear and then make it reappear again with a word. The chosen leader by a word destroys the coat; by a word re-creates it. His leadership is confirmed. He defeats the mother-goddess and from her body creates heaven and earth. What is the meaning of this test? If the male god is to match the strength of the goddess, he must have the one quality which makes her superior: the power to create. The test is to prove that he has this power as well as the characteristically masculine power to destroy the way in which man traditionally changed nature. He first destroys, then re-creates, a material object; but he does this with his word and not, like the woman, with her womb. Natural productivity is replaced by the magic of thought and word processes.

The biblical creation myth starts where the Babylonian myth ends. Almost all traces of the supremacy of a female goddess have now been eliminated. The creation starts with God's magic, the same magic of creation by word. The theme of male creation is repeated; contrary to fact, man is not born of woman, but she is made from him. The biblical myth is almost a song of triumph over defeated woman; it denies that women bear men and reverses the natural relations. In God's curse the supremacy of men is again upheld. The child-bearing function of women is recognized, but it is to be painful. Man is destined to work, that is to say to produce; thus he replaces the original productivity of the woman, even if this too is to be done in sweat and sorrow.

We have dealt at some length with the phenomenon of matriarchal remnants in the history of religion to illustrate one point that matters: the fact that the woman has the capacity of natural productiveness which the man lacks; that the man on this level is sterile. In certain periods of history this superiority of woman was consciously felt; later on, all the emphasis was on the magic and rational productivity of man. Nevertheless, it seems that unconsciously, even today, this difference has not entirely lost its meaning; somewhere in the man exists an awe of the woman for this capacity which he lacks. He is envious of it and fearful of it. Somewhere in his character is the need for a constant compensatory effort for his lack; somewhere in the woman, a feeling of superiority over him for his "sterility."

Thus far, we have dealt with certain characterological differences between men and women which have resulted from their sexual differences. Is this to be taken to mean that traits like overdependence, on the one hand, and craving for prestige and competitiveness, on the other, are essentially caused by the sex differences? Are "a" woman and "a" man to be expected to exhibit these traits, so that if they have the traits characteristic of the other sex this fact is to be explained by the presence of a homosexual component?

No conclusions of the kind follow. The sexual difference colors the personality of the average man and woman. This coloring may be compared to the key or the mode in which a melody is written—not to the melody itself. Furthermore, it refers only to the average man and woman respectively and varies in every person. These "natural" differences are blended with differences brought about by the specific culture in which people live. For instance, in our present-day culture, both in fact and in ideology, women are dependent on men and the craving for prestige and competitive success is found in men, but the presence of these trends has much less to do with sexual roles than with social roles. Society is organized in a way that necessarily produces these strivings, regardless of whether or not they have had roots in specific masculine or feminine peculiarities. The craving for prestige as it has been found in modern man since the end of the Middle Ages is chiefly conditioned by the social and economic system, not by his sexual role; the same is true of the dependency of women. What happens is that cultural patterns and social forms can create characterological trends that run parallel to identical tendencies rooted in entirely different sources, such as sexual differences. If that is the case, the two parallel trends are blended into one, and it seems as if these sources were also one. On the other hand, if the cultural patterns produce dependency in men, for instance, then this trend insofar as it results from sexual differences will be virtually eliminated from women and will be found in the sex opposite the one where it should be found according to "natural" differences.

The cravings for prestige and dependency, as products of culture, determine the whole personality; they are not its key, but the melody itself; then a woman is dependent, and a man is eager for prestige. The individual personality is thus reduced to one segment of the whole gamut of human personality. But the characterological differences as they spring from natural differences are not of this kind. The woman is not naturally dependent, the man is not vain. The reason for this may be found in the fact that deeper than the difference between the sexes is their equality, the fact that men and women are first of all human beings sharing the same potentialities, the same desires, and the same fears. Whatever is different in them on account of natural differences does not make them different. It gives their personalities, which are fundamentally alike, slight differences in the emphasis of one or another trend—an emphasis that appears empirically as a coloring. These differences, which are rooted in sexual differences, would seem to afford no basis for casting men and women in different roles in any given society.

It is apparent today that, whatever differences exist between the sexes, they are relatively insignificant in comparison with the characterological differences that are found between persons of the same sex. The sexual differences do not influence the capacity to do work of any kind. Certain highly differentiated achievements may be colored in their quality by sexual characteristics—one sex may be somewhat more gifted for a certain kind of work than is the other—but such is the case if extroverts are compared with introverts or pyknic with asthenic types. No one thinks of social, economic, and political differentiation according to such characteristics.

Again, in comparison with the general social influences which shape the masculine or feminine patterns, it is clear that the individual and, from a social standpoint, accidental experiences of any person are highly significant. These personal experiences in their turn blend themselves with the cultural patterns, mostly reinforcing but sometimes reducing their effects. The influence of the social and personal factors can scarcely but exceed in strength that of the "natural" ones which have been discussed here.

It is a sad commentary on the times that one feels the need of emphasizing that the differences due to the male or female role scarcely lend themselves to any judgment of value from a social or a moral point of view. They are neither good nor bad, neither desirable nor unfortunate, in and of themselves. The same trait will appear as a positive feature in one personality when certain conditions are present and as a negative feature in another personality when other conditions are present. Thus, the negative forms in which man's fear of failure and his need for prestige can appear are obvious: vanity, lack of seriousness, unreliability, and boastfulness. But it seems no less obvious that the very same trait can result in very positive character traits: initiative, activity, and courage. The same holds true with regard to the female characteristics as described. The woman's peculiar characteristics can, and often do, result in her inability to "stand on her own feet" practically, emotionally, and intellectually; but, given other conditions, she becomes the source of patience, reliability, intensity of love, development of erotic charm.

The positive or negative outcome of the one or the other characteristic depends on the whole of the character structure of the person with whom one is dealing. Such personality factors making for a positive or negative outcome are, for instance, anxiety versus self-reliance, or destructiveness versus constructiveness, respectively. But it is not sufficient to single out one or two of the more isolated traits; only the whole of the character structure determines whether one of the masculine or feminine characteristics turns into a positive or negative trait. This principle is the same which Klages has introduced in his system of graphology. Any single trait in the handwriting can have a positive or a negative meaning according to what he calls the Formniveau (the level of form) of the whole personality. If somebody's character can be called "orderly" it can mean one of two things: either it indicates something positive, namely, that he is not "sloppy," that he is capable of organizing his life; or it can mean something negative, namely, that he is pedantic, sterile, or without initiative. Obviously the trait orderliness is at the root of both the negative and positive outcomes, but the outcome is determined by a number of other factors in the total personality; these, in their turn, depend on external conditions which make for growth or for a thwarting of life, respectively.

Although the relationship of superiority-inferiority implies at least momentary difference, that difference is by no means identical with, or necessarily at all related to, superiority-inferiority. Those who cannot realize this are people who on the basis of their whole personality structure are incapable of understanding or of experiencing equality. Thus, the fascist-authoritarian character cannot but confuse difference with inequality. He is influenced in his thinking by his contempt for anyone who has less power than himself and by his "love" for one who is powerful. A human relationship based on respect for the dignity of every person simply escapes him. Whenever he senses differences he has to seek for an implied superiority or inferiority. Insofar as he can show differences between groups, he believes that he has proved that one is superior to the other. Those who hold to the principle of human equality should not be misled into accepting this fascist premise. Social conditions can be created which will develop the positive side of the peculiarities of persons, sexes, and national groups. These conditions are needed all over the world. If they are realized, those differences of one person from another will be accentuated—which are not matters of the good or bad but rather the individual colorings of personality—making for a richer and broader human culture and a more integrated family structure.

# 7

## Man–Woman (1951)

The problem of the relationship between men and women is obviously exceedingly difficult, for if it were not, people wouldn't be mismanaging it as frequently as they do. So the best thing to do in discussing it is to try to raise some questions. If through these questions I can provoke your own thinking, perhaps you will be able to give some answers from your experience.

The first question I want to raise is: Does not the topic itself imply a fallacy? It seems to imply that the difficulties in the relationship between man and woman are essentially due to the difference in sex. That is not so. The relationship between man and woman—men and women—is essentially a relationship between human beings. Whatever is good in the relationship between one human being and another is good in the relationship between men and women, and whatever is bad in human relationships is bad in the relationship between men and women.

The particular defects in the relationship between men and

116

women are largely not specific to their male and female characteristics, but to their person-to-person human relationships. I shall come back to this problem a little later, but I want to make a second qualification of this whole topic. The relationship between men and women is a relationship between a victorious and a defeated group. This may sound strange and funny in the United States in the year 1949; yet we have to consider the history of the relationship between men and women in the last five thousand years to understand how history colors the present-day situation and the present-day attitude between the sexes and what they know and feel about each other. Only then can we approach the question of how, specifically, men and women differ; only then can we determine what is characteristic of the relationship between men and women and what is a problem in its own right and not a problem merely of human relationships.

Let me start out with this second question, defining the relationship between men and women as the relationship between a victorious and a defeated group. I said it sounds funny to say this in the United States at this day and age because quite obviously women, certainly in the big cities, don't look and don't feel and don't act like a defeated group.

There has been a good deal of discussion, and not without reason, as to which is the stronger sex in our urban culture today. I do not think the problem is as simple as all that, however. It isn't even as simple as the statement that in America women have accomplished their emancipation and therefore are on equal footing with men makes it appear. I think the struggle of many thousands of years still shows in the particular way in which the relationship between men and women in our culture is maintained.

There is some good evidence for assuming that the patriarchal society as it existed in China, in India, and in Europe and America for the last five thousand to six thousand years is not

117

the only form in which the two sexes have organized their lives. There is a good deal of evidence that (if not everywhere, at any rate in many places) the patriarchal societies dominated by men were preceded by matriarchal societies. These were characterized by the fact that the woman and mother was the center of society and of the family.

Woman was dominant in the social system and in the family system, and you can see the traces of her dominance in the various religious systems. You find the traces of this old organization even in a document with which we all are familiar, the Old Testament.

If you read the story of Adam and Eve with some objectivity, what do you find? You find that a curse is pronounced against Eve; and indirectly against Adam, because to dominate others is not better than to be dominated. As a punishment for her sin, man shall rule over her, and her desire shall be to her husband.

It is obvious that if the domination of men over women is established as a new principle, there must have been a time when this was not so, and indeed we have documents which show that this was the case. If you compare the Babylonian account of the creation with the biblical story you find that in this Babylonian story, which antecedes the biblical story in time, something quite different existed. In the center of the Babylonian account you find not a masculine god but a goddess, Tiamat. Her sons tried to rebel against her and eventually defeated her and established the rule of male gods under the leadership of Marduk, the great Babylonian god.

If you read the biblical story of creation you will find that it begins where the Babylonian story ends. God creates the world by his word; and in order to emphasize the superiority of patriarchal over matriarchal culture, the Bible story tells us that Eve was created from a man rather than that man was born of woman.

The patriarchal culture, the culture in which men appear to be destined to rule over women, to be the stronger sex, has persisted all over the world. In fact, only in small primitive communities today do we find certain remnants of the older matriarchal form. It is only very recently that man's rule over woman has been breaking down.

Whether a matriarchal or patriarchal system is better is hard to say. In fact, I think the question in this form is wrong because you might say that the matriarchal system emphasizes the elements of natural ties, of natural equality, of love; and the patriarchal system then emphasizes the elements of civilization, of thought, of the state, of invention and industries and, in many ways, of progress, in comparison with the old matriarchal culture.

The aim of mankind must be not to have any kind of hierarchy, either matriarchal or patriarchal. We must come to a situation in which the sexes relate to each other without any attempt to dominate. Only in that way can they develop their real differences, their real polarity.

It is important to recognize that our cultural system is not, even though it seems so, the fulfillment of this goal. It is the end of patriarchal domination, but it is not yet a system in which the two sexes meet each other as equals. There is a great deal of fighting going on. I am convinced that this fight is to some extent not simply an individual fight between two people, but is still connected with an age-old fight between the sexes. It is the continuing conflict of a male and a female who are confused and don't quite know what each one's role is.

In patriarchal society there existed all the typical ideologies and prejudices that a ruling group always develops regarding those whom they rule: women are emotional, they are undisciplined, they are vain, they are like children, they are not good organizers, and they are not as strong as men—but they are charming.

Yet it is obvious that these ideas about the nature of women which were developed in patriarchal societies are, in some instances, the very opposite of true. Whence the idea that women are more vain than men? I think anyone who studies man can see that if there is anything that can be said about men it is that they are vain. In fact, they hardly do anything without some element of wanting to show off.

Women are far less vain than men are. It is true enough that women are sometimes forced to show some vanity because they either are or were in the position of those who have to seek favors, being the so-called weaker sex; but certainly the legend that women are more vain than men are is disproved by any dispassionate observation.

Take another prejudice: take the idea that men are tougher than women are. Every nurse can tell you that the percentage of men fainting when they get an injection or a blood test is much greater than the percentage of women, that women on the whole are much better able to endure pain which turns men into helpless children and makes them run to mother. Yet men over the centuries, or rather over thousands of years, have succeeded in spreading the idea that they are the stronger and the tougher sex.

Well, there is nothing surprising about that. It is the typical ideology of a group of people who have to prove that they have a right to rule. If you are not in the majority but almost exactly half of the human race, and have claimed for thousands of years that you have a right to rule over the other half, then your ideologies must be plausible in order to convince the other half, and particularly in order to convince yourself.

In the eighteenth and nineteenth centuries the problem of equality between men and women really became acute. A very interesting phenomenon developed during that period—namely, that those who claimed that women should have equal rights with men also claimed that there was no difference between the two sexes psychologically. As the French formulated it, the soul is sexless; there is no psychological difference whatsoever. Those who were against the political and social equality of women emphasized, often very intelligently and subtly, how different women were from men psychologically. Of course the point they came to again and again was that because of the psychological differences women were better off and fulfilled their destiny better if they did not participate in social and political life on an equal footing.

Even up to this day we find a similar attitude among many feminists, progressives, liberals, or any group who are in favor of equality between human beings in general and between the two sexes specifically; those of this attitude claim that there are no differences, or minimize these differences. They say that whatever differences exist, they are due only to cultural environment and to education, and that there are no intrinsic psychological differences between the sexes that are not the result of such environmental or educational factors.

I am afraid that this viewpoint, which is so popular among the defenders of the equality of men and women, is a bad one in many ways. Perhaps its worst fault is that it isn't true. It is about the same as saying that there are no psychological differences among various national groups and that anyone who uses the word *race* is then and there saying something terrible. While it may very well be that scientifically the word *race* is not a good word, it is true that there are differences in body and temperament among the peoples of various nations.

The second reason I think this kind of reasoning is bad is that it suggests false principles. It suggests that equality implies that everyone is like everybody else, that equality implies identity. Actually, equality and the demand for equality imply the very opposite, namely, that despite all differences no person should be made a tool of the purpose of anyone else, that every

121

human being is an end and purpose in himself or herself. This means that each person is free to develop his or her peculiarity as an individual, as a member of a given sex, as a member of a given nationality. Equality does not imply the negation of difference but the possibility for its fullest realization.

If we imply that equality means that there are no differences, we shall fortify the very tendencies which lead to the impoverishment of our culture—that is, to the "automatization" of individuals and the weakening of that which is the most valuable part of human existence, the unfolding and development of the peculiarities of each person.

In using the word *peculiarities* I should like to remind you how strange a fate this word has had. If we say today that someone is peculiar, we don't mean anything particularly pleasant. Yet this should be the greatest compliment we can pay. Saying that someone is peculiar should mean that he has not given in, that he has retained the most valuable part of human existence, his individuality, that he is a unique person, different from anyone else under the sun.

I think that in America the fallacy of assuming that equality is synonymous with identity is one of the reasons for this peculiar phenomenon in our culture: the differences between the sexes tend to be minimized, tend to be covered up, tend to be argued away. Women try to be like men, men sometimes like women, and the polarity between male and female, between men and women, tends to disappear.

Indeed, I believe that the only answer to the problem, speaking in somewhat general terms, is to work toward a concept of polarity in the relationship between the two sexes. You would not say of the positive or negative pole of an electric current that one is inferior to the other. You would say that the field between them is caused by their polarity, and that this very polarity is the basis of productive forces.

In the same sense the two sexes and that for which they stand (the male and the female aspect in the world, in the universe, and in each of us) are two poles that have to retain their difference, their polarity, in order to exercise the fruitful dynamism, the productive force, that springs from that very polarity.

Let me come now to the second premise that the relationship between men and women is never better than the relationship between human beings in any given society, and never worse, either. If I were to single out in our interpersonal relations that which most affects and damages relations between men and women, I should speak of what in my book *Man for Himself* I called the marketing orientation. I should speak of the fact that we all are terribly alone, even though on the surface we are all so social and have "contacts" with so many people.

The average person today is terribly alone and feels alone. He feels himself to be a commodity, by which I mean he feels that his value depends on his success, depends on his saleability, depends on approval by others. He feels that it does not depend on the intrinsic or what you might call *use value* of his personality, not on his powers, not on his capacity to love, not on his human qualities—except if he can sell them, except if he can be successful, except if he is approved by others. This is what I mean by the "marketing orientation."

This accounts for the fact that the self-esteem of most people today is very shaky. They do not feel themselves worthy because of their own conviction: "This is me, this is my capacity to love, this is my capacity to think and to feel," but because they are approved by others, because they can sell themselves, because others say: "This is a wonderful man" or "a wonderful woman."

Naturally, when the feeling of self-esteem is dependent upon others it becomes uncertain. Each day is a new battle because each day you have to convince someone, and you have to prove to yourself, that you are all right.

To use an analogy, I would suggest that you consider how handbags would feel on a counter in a store. The handbag of one particular style, of which many have been sold, would feel elated in the evening; and the other handbag, of a style a little out of fashion or a little too expensive or which, for some reason or other, had not been sold, would be depressed.

The one handbag would feel: "I am wonderful," and the other handbag would feel: "I am unworthy," and yet the "wonderful" handbag may not be more beautiful or more useful or have any better intrinsic quality than the other one. The unsold handbag would feel it was not wanted. In our analogy, a handbag's sense of value would depend on its success, on how many purchasers, for one reason or another, preferred the one to the other.

In human terms that means that one must be peculiar, that one's own personality must be always open to change in order to conform to the latest model. That is why parents often feel embarrassed when they are with their children. The children know the latest model better than the parents do. But the parents are very ready to be taught, to be told, to learn. They, like the children, listen to the latest quotations on the personality market.

And where do you find these market quotations? Where do you read them? In the movies, in the liquor ads, in the clothing ads, in the indications of the ways that important people dress and talk.

A model is considered outmoded after only a few years. I read in the *Sunday Times Magazine* of a little girl of fourteen who said that her mother was so old-fashioned that she still thought it was 1945. At first I didn't understand. I thought it was a misprint until I understood that for this girl 1945 seemed awfully out-of-date. But I am sure her mother knew, nevertheless, that she had to hurry.

How does this "marketing orientation" affect the relationship between the sexes, between men and women? I think, in the first place, that a great deal of what goes under the name of love is this seeking for success, for approval. One needs someone to tell one not only at four o'clock in the afternoon but also at eight and at ten and at twelve: "You're fine, you're all right, you are doing well." That is one factor.

The other factor is that one also proves one's value by choosing the right person. One needs to be the latest model oneself, but one then has a right also and a duty to fall in love with the latest model. That can be put as crudely as it was put by a boy of eighteen who was asked what the ambition of his life was. He said be wanted to buy a better car; he wanted to change from a Ford to a Buick so that he could pick up a better class of girls.

Well, this boy was at least frank, but I think he expressed something that, in a more subtle way, determines the choice of partners to a large extent in our culture.

The marketing orientation has another effect on the relationship between the sexes. In the marketing orientation everything is patterned, and we are eager to live up to the latest model and to act in the latest way. Accordingly the roles we choose, particularly our sex roles, are highly patterned, but the patterns are not even or uniform. Frequently they are conflicting. Man ought to be aggressive in business and tender at home. He ought to live for his work but not be tired in the evening when be comes home. He ought to be ruthless with his customers or competitors, but he ought to be very honest with his wife and children. He ought to be liked by everyone, and yet he should have the deepest feeling for his family.

Well! The poor man tries to live up to these patterns. Only the fact that he does not take them too seriously probably protects him from going crazy. The same holds true with women. They too have to live patterns that are as contradictory as those for the males.

There always were, of course, in every culture, patterns for what was considered to be male and female, masculine and feminine; but formerly these patterns had at least a certain stability. In a culture in which we depend so much on the latest pattern, on being just right, on approval, on fitting in with what is expected, the real qualities that belong to our male or female roles become obscured. Very little specific is left in the relationship between men and women.

If the choices in relationships between men and women are made on the basis of market orientation, of highly patterned roles, one thing must happen: people get bored. I think that the word *bored* does not get the attention it deserves. We speak of all sorts of terrible things that happen to people, but we rarely speak about one of the most terrible things of all: that is, being bored, being bored alone and, worse than that, being bored together.

Many people see only two solutions for this boredom. They avoid being bored by using any of the many avenues our culture offers. They go to parties, make contacts, drink, play cards, listen to the radio, and so kid themselves every day, every evening. Or—and this is partly a matter of to what social class they belong—they think things are changed by a change of partner. The think this or that marriage was no good because they got the wrong partner, and they suppose that a change of partner will dispel boredom.

People do not see that the main question is not: "Am I loved?" which is to a large extent the question: "Am I approved of? Am I protected? Am I admired?" The main question is: "Can I love?"

That is indeed difficult. To be loved and to "fall in love" is very simple for a while until you get boring and bored. But to love, "to stand in love," as it were, is indeed difficult, although not superhuman; in fact, it is the most essential human quality.

If one cannot be alone with oneself, if one cannot be genuinely interested in others and in oneself, then one cannot be together with anyone else without being bored after a certain time. If the relationship between the sexes becomes a refuge for the loneliness and isolation of the individual, it has very little to do with the potentialities that the real relationship between male and female implies.

There is another fallacy I want to mention. That is the fallacy that the real problem between the sexes is sex. We felt very proud thirty years ago, or many of us did, when during the era of sexual emancipation it seemed that the chains of the past were breaking and that a new phase of human relations between the sexes was opening up. Yet the results were not so wonderful as many thought they would be, because all that glitters isn't sex. There are many motivations for the sexual urge that in themselves are not sexual.

Vanity is one of the greatest stimuli for sex, much more than anything else, perhaps; but so is loneliness, so is rebelliousness against an existing relationship. A man who is driven to make new sexual conquests thinks he is motivated by the sexual attraction women have for him, but actually he is motivated by his vanity, by the drive to prove that he is superior to all other males.

No sexual relationship is better than the human relationship between the two people. Sex is very often a shortcut to closeness, but it is very deceptive. While sex is certainly a part of human relationships, it is in our culture so overburdened with all sorts of other functions that I am afraid that what appears as great sexual freedom is by no means exclusively a matter of sex.

Well then, do we know anything about the real differences between men and women? What I have said so far has been negative. If you expected a clear statement of the differences between men and women, you must be disappointed. I don't think we know them. We could not possibly know them in view of the circumstances I mentioned before. If the two sexes have fought for thousands of years, if they have developed prejudices against each other which are characteristic of such fighting situations, how could we possibly at this point know what the real differences are?

Only if we forget about the differences, if we forget about the stereotypes, can we develop a sense of that equality to which each person is an end in himself or herself. Then we might learn something about the differences between men and women.

I should like to mention one difference, however, which I think has a certain relevance to the success of man–woman relationships and so ought to be considered in our culture. It seems to me that women are probably more capable of being tender than men. This is not surprising, because in woman's relationship to her child tenderness to the child is the main virtue.

It is the fashion today, as you all know, especially if you hear psychiatric lectures, to emphasize that it matters a great deal when the child is weaned, when it is nursed, and how the toilet training proceeds, and people believe their prescriptions for making a child happy by all these little techniques are effective.

What people forget is that there is only one thing that matters, and that is the tenderness of a mother for her child, and tenderness implies a great deal. Tenderness implies love, tenderness implies respect, tenderness implies knowledge. Tenderness, by its very nature, is something quite different from sex or hunger or thirst. You might say, psychologically speaking, that such drives as sex and hunger and thirst are characterized by a self-propelling dynamism; they become more and more intense and end in a rather sudden climax in which satisfaction is achieved and nothing more is wanted, for the moment.

This is the nature of one type of craving or drive. Tenderness belongs to another type of striving. Tenderness is not self-propelling, it has no aim, it has no climax, it has no end. Its satisfaction is in the very act itself, in the joy of being friendly, of being warm, of considering and respecting another person and of making this other person happy. I think tenderness is one of the most self-assertive, joyful experiences anyone can have, and human beings are generally capable of it. For such people there is nothing selfless about it, there is nothing sacrificial about it. It is only sacrificial for the person who cannot be tender.

I have an impression that we have little tenderness in our culture. Take the love stories in the movies. All the passionate kisses are censored out, and yet the audience is supposed to imagine how wonderful they are. The movies allegedly describe passion. They may not be too convincing to many; but to many others this is what is supposed to be love. But how often do you find in the movies an expression of real tenderness between the sexes? or between adults and children? or between human beings in general? I think very seldom. By this I do not mean to say that we do not have the capacity for tenderness, but that tenderness is discouraged in our culture. The reason for this is partly that our culture is one that is purpose-oriented. Everything has a purpose; everything has an aim and should lead somewhere; you must "get somewhere."

It is true enough that we try to save time—then we don't know what we should do with it, so we kill it. But our first impulse is to get somewhere. We have very little feeling for the process of living itself without getting anywhere, just living, just eating or drinking or sleeping or thinking or feeling or seeing something. If living has no purpose, we say, what good is it? Tenderness has no purpose either. Tenderness has not the physiological purpose of relief or sudden satisfaction that sex has. It has no purpose except the enjoyment of a feeling of warmth, pleasure, and care for another person.

So we discourage tenderness. People, especially men, feel uncomfortable when they show tenderness. Furthermore, the very attempt to deny differences between the sexes, the very attempt to make men and women as alike as possible, has prevented women from showing the amount of tenderness of which they are capable and which is specifically feminine.

Here I come back to where I started, to my point that the battle between the sexes is not over. Women in America have achieved a great deal of equality. This equality is not complete, but it is much more than it used to be. Yet women still have to defend this achievement. Therefore they have to be very eager, to prove that they have a right to equality by being as different as possible from men. And therefore they suppress impulses to tenderness. The result is that men miss tenderness, and as a substitute for it they feel they ought to be admired, and that their self-esteem ought to be validated. So they are in a state of constant dependence and fear; and women are in a state of frustration because they are not allowed to play the role of their own sex with full freedom.

This is certainly an overdrawn picture, and if you say that this is not always so, that it is not fair to insist on it, I would quite agree with you; but, after all, in order to generalize you have to overdraw the picture for the moment.

To conclude these remarks about the relationship between men and women, I would emphasize again that in order to know the difference between them, one must forget about it. One must permit oneself to live fully and spontaneously as a human being and not become preoccupied with the questions: Am I the typical male or the typical female? Do I fit the role prescribed by the culture? Am I successful in my sex role? Only if one forgets such questions, only then will the profound polarity that exists between the sexes and within every human being develop into a productive force.

# III

## Gender and Sexuality

# 8

## Sexuality and Character (1948)

Freud's theory of sex, first published in the beginning of this century, was a challenge to a generation which still had an unshaken belief in the sex taboos of the Victorian age. Freud had shown that the stigmatization of sex resulting in guilt feelings was conducive to neurosis. Furthermore, he had demonstrated that deviations from the so-called normal sexual behavior were not rare monstrosities but a part of the normal sexual development from infancy to adolescence and that the sexual aberrations in the adult were remnants of earlier sexual patterns and ought to be understood as neurotic symptoms rather than morally condemned as vices.

In view of the fact that Freud and his school put sexuality into the center of their psychological theory, it is all the more amazing that an extensive survey of sexual behavior has not been undertaken by psychoanalysts prior to Kinsey's report in 1948. One would imagine that his report would be highly welcome to all psychoanalysts as a report on facts which support the general trend of the psychoanalytic position, even though this report deals only with manifest behavior and not with the problem of unconscious motivations and character. However, quite in contrast to this expectation, the Kinsey Report has been received with unfriendly criticism by a number of psychoanalysts (a minority only, I hope). One criticism, for instance, goes as far as asserting that Kinsey could not possibly have unearthed such wealth of data in so short a time when, in contrast, psychoanalysts found it very difficult to gather comparative data about one individual even in numerous interviews. Such an argument, indeed, can always be used if one researcher is more successful than his predecessors, but it is obviously not a valid criticism.

In examining the significance of the Kinsey Report from the standpoint of the psychoanalyst, we must first consider the theoretical differences of psychoanalytic schools with regard to the role of sex in human behavior. Freud and his followers assumed that the energy source of human behavior was largely sexual. The assumption was made that the normal development of the libido can be arrested or distorted by the impact of environmental influences, particularly those in early childhood, and that peculiarities of behavior and of character in the adult were rooted in the peculiarities of his sexual desires and aims. The characteristics of a person's sexual life were held to be exemplary for his total personality.

Sadistic strivings, for instance, are a case in point. Freud assumed that sadistic impulses were part of the sexual strivings in the child during a certain period of its development. Provided that this early phase of the child's sexual development remained predominant in his sexual life, he would, as an adult, either develop sadism as a sexual perversion or as a character structure in which the desire to overpower, dominate, and belittle his fellow men is paramount.

Another illustration is that of "oral cravings." Freud assumed that before the sexual drive has become focused on the genitals it finds expression in more diffuse ways in connection with other bodily zones. In this view the infant is characterized by the predominance of libidinous pleasure connected with the mouth and its functions of drinking and eating. If this phase of sexual organization becomes fixated, behavior of the adult will still be determined by this underlying oral craving. Such a person will tend "to be fed" and supported by others, to be dependent on them, to want to be taken care of, and to remain essentially passive.

Freud's assumption is that a person's attitude toward others is a sublimation of (or a "reaction formation" against) those sexual strivings which are the dominant ones in his personality; that it is the particular kind of sexual adjustment which determines the emotional adjustment and the kind of interpersonal relationship the individual develops.

Freud tried to account for the dynamic nature of character traits by combining his characterology with his libido theory. In accordance with the type of materialistic thinking prevalent in the natural sciences of the late nineteenth century, which assumed that energy was a substantial rather than a relational concept, Freud believed that the sexual drive was the source of energy for the formation of character. By a number of complicated and brilliant assumptions he explained different character traits as "sublimations" of, or "reaction formations" against, the various forms of the sexual drive. He interpreted the dynamic nature of character traits as an expression of their libidinous source.

The development of psychoanalytic theory led, parallel to the development in the natural sciences emphasizing dynamic interrelations, to a new concept which was based on the relationship of man to others, to nature, and to himself, discarding the older concept of an isolated individual, a "homo psychologicus." This concept was very adequately formulated by H. S. Sullivan in defining psychoanalysis as a "study in interpersonal relations." (Cf. H. S. Sullivan 1940 and 1945) Interpersonal relationships, assumed by Freud to be the result of varying forms of sexual desire, are considered to be the factor determining sexual strivings. In this view it is not sexual behavior that determines character, but character that determines sexual behavior.

A few illustrations may help to understand this "relational" concept. If the dominant trait in a person's character is that of manipulating other people as "things" to be used for one's own purposes (cf. my description of the "marketing orientation" in Fromm 1947a), his sexual attitude will be in accordance with this character trait. This person experiences others as a means of satisfying his sexual needs and at best his principle is that of "fair play," an exchange in which neither partner gives more than he receives. In this character orientation sexual relations are experienced as a fair exchange rather than as intimate relatedness and love.

The authoritarian character, whose relation to others is determined by his wish for power and domination, shows the same characteristics also in his sexual attitude, ranging from complete disregard for the sexual partner to pleasure in inflicting physical or emotional pain. In the submissive person, on the other hand, the masochistic tendency to suffer and to be dominated is a character trait which determines his sexual behavior and often results in impotence and frigidity.

The character orientations which I have just discussed show how sexual aberrations are rooted in a person's character structure. The buying of "love," and sadistic and masochistic perversion are determined by the dominant traits in a person's character just as sexual happiness is based on the person's capacity for love. In the productive person who is capable of relating himself to another person not in terms of "buying" or of conquest and defeat but in terms of equality and mutual respect, sexual desire is an expression and fulfillment of love.

The fact that sexual behavior is determined by character is not in contradiction to the fact that the sexual instinct itself is rooted in the chemistry of our body. This instinct is the root of all forms of sexual behavior, but it is the particular way of satisfying it, not the instinct itself, which is determined by the character structure, by the particular kind of person's relatedness to the world.

Sexual behavior, indeed, offers one of the most distinct clues for the understanding of a person's character. In contrast to almost every other activity, sexual activity by its very nature is private and therefore less patterned and more an expression of individual peculiarities. Furthermore, the intensity of the sexual desire makes sexual behavior less amenable to a person's control.

Thus, while Freud's description of the connection between sexual behavior and character remains valid, our explanation is different. As so often happens in the history of thought the development of theoretical insight is not to be found in the negation of an older theory, but in its reinterpretation. In our view sexual behavior is not the cause but the effect of a person's character structure. Hence, the Kinsey Report, with its wealth of data on sexual behavior, constitutes an invaluable source of information for the student of social psychology and particularly of character.

For centuries sexuality had been stigmatized as morally bad and at best as morally indifferent if sanctioned by the sacrament of marriage. Every sexual activity which was not for the purpose of procreation, and particularly all sexual deviations, were considered to be morally evil. The general assumption underlying this attitude was that man's flesh was a source of corruption and that only by suppressing instinctual demands could goodness be achieved.

Against these moral concepts a rebellion has developed since the beginning of our century, stimulated by the works of men like Freud and Havelock Ellis. Freud pointed to the fact that the suppression of sex frequently led to the development of neurosis. He accused his culture of sacrificing mental health to the demands of puritan morality. But it seems that another effect of sexual taboos is not less important: the development of intense guilt feelings in every individual. Since every normal human being has sexual strivings from childhood on, these very strivings must become an inexhaustible source of guilt feelings if they are stigmatized by the culture as evil. Guilt feelings make a person prone to submit to authorities which want to use and subdue him for their own ends. Indeed, maturity and happiness conflict with the existence of an all-pervasive sense of guilt.

The stigmatization of sex had another most undesirable result: ethics was narrowed down to the small area of sexual behavior, and thus the really significant ethical problems in human behavior were veiled. Morality became almost identified with sexual morality and virtue, with the obedience to the sexual taboos postulated by the culture. Thus the decisive problem of ethics, of man's relatedness to his fellow men, was neglected. Lack of love, indifference, envy, and lust for power were considered to be less significant ethical problems than the respect for sexual conventions. The issue of ethics was befogged by the idea that man's "flesh" was the source of evil. Yet if one studies the history of man, it is not difficult to see that those human traits which are a threat to the peace and happiness of society and of the individual are not sexual passions or other appetites rooted in our physiological makeup, but the irrational "mental" passions like hate, envy, and ambition. Indeed, all physical instinctual appetites, including sex, are harmless even in their deviations and perversions and are no threat to the welfare of the human race in comparison with the damage done by those irrational passions just mentioned.

But while the rebellion against the suppression of sex was a healthy and progressive development it went to the opposite extreme; it arrived at an equally untenable position by maintaining that sexual behavior does not lend itself to any kind of ethical evaluation.

However, if our behavior and feeling toward our fellow men are the subject matter of ethics, how could sexual behavior— one of the most significant expressions of a person's relatedness to others—be excluded from the realm of ethical judgment? If we believe that love, respect, and responsibility for others are fundamental ethical values, sexual behavior must be judged in terms of these values. Inasmuch as the particular form of sexual satisfaction is rooted in a person's character it can be judged as any other characterologically significant behavior.

An example of the connection between sexual behavior and genuine ethical problems is the most ancient and universal sexual taboo, the incest taboo, as we find it in various forms in all primitive cultures as well as in our own. But even today the prohibition of incest has retained its taboo quality and has not been connected with the problem of character and of rational ethics. If it were true, as most people assume, that incest is a rare perversion which has little relevance in our own culture, there would be no need for discussing this problem. But while it is true that incest in the crude form of sexual desires between relatives is comparatively rare, it becomes a very acute problem, indeed, if we understand how incestuous desires are rooted in our character.

Incestuous love can be understood here as a symbol. It symbolizes the inability to love "the stranger," that is, a person with whom we are not "familiar" and not related by ties of blood and early intimacy. Its supplement is xenophobia, the hate and distrust of "the stranger." Incest is a symbol of the warmth and security of the womb and of the dependence on the navel-string in contradistinction to mature independence. Only if one can love "the stranger," only if one can recognize and relate oneself to the human core of another person can one experience oneself as a human being, and only if one can experience oneself as a human individuality can one love "the stranger." We have overcome incest in the narrow sense of the word, as sexual relations between members of the same family, but we still practice incest not in a sexual but in a character-ological sense, inasmuch as we are not capable of loving "the stranger," a person with different social background. Race and nationalistic prejudices are the symptoms of incestuous elements in our contemporary culture. We shall have overcome incest only when we—every one of us—are able not only to think of but to feel and to accept the stranger as our brother.

The problem of incest may suffice as an illustration for what I want to say about the general problem of the relationship between ethics and sexual desires. Here, as with regard to many other sexual problems, it is not sexuality as such but the implied basic attitude to other human beings which is ethically significant. We have to undertake a reevaluation of the moral aspects of sex. Both the moral condemnation of sexuality and the reaction to it, the position of complete ethical relativism in matters of sex, have failed as guiding principles. By under-standing the psychological significance of sexual behavior with regard to the total personality, we can recognize that sexual behavior is subject to ethical value judgments.

The problem of sex and happiness is closely related to the ethical problem we have just discussed. To the assumption that the suppression of sex was not only the basis of virtue but also the condition for happiness, the reaction was that sexual sat-isfaction was the paramount condition for happiness if not identical with it. Freud and his school emphasized that sexual satisfaction was one condition for mental health and happiness. Today it is widely advocated and believed that marital happiness is based primarily on sexual satisfaction and that marital unhappiness can be cured by applying better sexual techniques. However, the facts do not seem to bear out these assumptions. True enough, many neuroses are coupled with sexual disturbances and many unhappy people suffer also from sexual frustrations; but it is not true that sexual satisfaction is the cause of—or identical with—mental health and happiness. Often psychoanalysts see patients whose ability to love and so be close to others is damaged and yet who function very well sexually and indeed make sexual satisfaction a substitute for love because their sexual potency is their only power in which they have confidence. Their inability to be productive in all other spheres of life and the resulting unhappiness is counterbalanced and veiled by their sexual activities. The meaning of sexual desires and their satisfaction can be determined only with reference to the character structure. Sexual desires can be the expression of fear, vanity, or of a wish for domination, and they can be the expression of love. The question whether sexual satisfaction is conducive to happiness depends entirely on its role within the total character structure.

The discussion of the relationship between sexual satisfaction and happiness even in the sketchy form of this paper must pay attention to a fundamental controversy with regard to the concept of happiness. One view maintains that happiness must be defined entirely in subjective terms. In this view happiness is identical with the satisfaction of any kind of desire a person may have. Happiness is looked upon as a matter of taste and preference, irrespective of the quality of the particular desire. In contrast to this relativistic position, which is the dominant one today in the popular mind, the position represented in the tradition of humanistic philosophy, from Plato and Aristotle to Spinoza and Dewey, has emphasized that happiness, while not at all identical with obedience to norms given by an external authority, nevertheless is also not "relative" but subject to norms which follow from the nature of man. "Happiness is the indication that man has found the answer to the problem of human existence: the productive realization of his potentialities and thus, simultaneously, being one with the world and preserving the integrity of his self. In spending his energy productively he increases his powers, he *burns without being consumed.*

"Happiness is the criterion of excellence in the art of living, of virtue in the meaning it has in humanistic ethics." (Fromm 1947a, 189)

The assumption that happiness results from sexual satisfaction alone and not from our capacity to love tends to camouflage and to befog the issue just as much as the Victorian prejudice against sexual satisfaction did. In both instances sex is isolated from the total personality and considered good or evil in itself, while it can be evaluated only in the context of the total character structure. Mere negation of the Victorian moral code remains sterile.

"Happiness is not the reward of virtue, but is virtue itself; nor do we delight in happiness because we restrain our lusts; but, on the contrary, because we delight in it, therefore are we able to restrain them." (Spinoza, *Ethics*)

If we believe in the significance sexual behavior has for the understanding of character, the Kinsey Report must be considered of great importance for the study of "social character." By "social character" I refer to the core of the character common to most members of a culture, in contradistinction to the individual character, in which people belonging to the same culture differ from one another. A society is not something outside of the individuals which it is composed of, but it is the totality of these many individuals. The emotional forces which are operating in most of its members become powerful forces in the social process, stabilizing, changing, or disrupting it.

The study of the social character is the main topic of the problem of "personality and culture" which has become one focus of attention in contemporary social science. Unfortunately, progress in this field has been slow so far. One has relied much too exclusively on gathering data on what people think (or believe that they are supposed to think) instead of studying the emotional forces behind their thinking. While opinion polls are significant for certain purposes, we need to know more; they are not the tool for understanding the forces operating underneath the surface of opinion. Only if we know these forces are we able to predict how the members of a society will react in critical situations to those ideas which they profess to believe in and to new ideologies which they now reject. From the standpoint of social dynamics every opinion is worth only as much as the emotional matrix in which it is rooted.

But far from having a picture of the social character in its totality, we do not even have studies of the most urgent specific problems. What, for instance, do we know about happiness of people in our culture? True enough, many people would answer in an opinion poll that they were happy because this is what a self-respecting citizen is supposed to feel. But the degree of genuine happiness or unhappiness in our culture is anybody's guess, and yet it is this very knowledge which can answer the question whether our institutions fulfill the purpose they are devised for: the greatest happiness of the greatest number. Or what do we know about the degree of which ethical considerations and not mere fear of disapproval or punishment influence the behavior of modern man? Tremendous expenditures in energy and money are made to increase the weight of ethical motivations. Yet we know hardly anything, beyond mere guesswork, about the success of these efforts.

Or to take another illustration—what do we know of the degree and intensity of the destructive forces to be found in the average person in our culture? While it cannot be denied that our hopes for peaceful and democratic development depend largely on the assumption that the average man is not possessed by intense destructiveness, nothing has been done to ascertain the facts. The opinion that most people are basically destructive is as unproven as the opinion that the opposite is true. Social scientists so far have done little to shed light on this crucial issue.

The reason for the neglect to study these fundamental problems of character and culture is largely to be found in the attitude of most social psychologists. They believe that unless phenomena can be studied in a way which permits of exact and quantitative analysis they must not be studied at all. They try to imitate methods successful in natural sciences and make a fetish of "the" scientific method. Instead of devising new methods proper to the study of significant problems in their own field, namely, people and life processes, they choose those problems for study which fit the requirements of laboratory methods. Their choice of problems is determined by the method instead of the method being determined by the problem.

Kinsey's survey ought to be very stimulating to social scientists for two reasons: (1) Its data throw light on one aspect of behavior and hence, if properly interpreted, on the social character. (2) Kinsey has succeeded in unearthing relevant data in a field which was believed to be impenetrable. Although methods for studying the social character must necessarily differ from the quantitative-statistical method legitimately used by Kinsey for the study of sexual behavior, the difficulties in devising and applying proper methods for social characterology are not insurmountable. Empirical investigations studying the forces underlying mass behavior will yield significant results if social psychologists approach their problems with the same courage and energy which Kinsey and his collaborators have demonstrated in their work.

# 9

## Changing Concepts of Homosexuality (1940)

The term *homosexual* as used in psychoanalysis has come to be a kind of wastebasket into which are dumped all forms of relationships with one's own sex. The word may be applied to activities, attitudes, feelings, thoughts, or repression of any of these. In short, anything which pertains in any way to a relationship, hostile or friendly, to a member of one's own sex may be termed homosexual. Under the circumstances, what does an analyst convey to himself, his audience, or his patient when he says the patient has homosexual trends? It does not clarify much in his own thinking, nor convey a definite idea to his audience. When he uses the term in talking with the patient his words, instead of being helpful, often produce terror, for in ordinary speech the word *homosexual* has a much more specific meaning, and in addition a disturbing emotional coloring. In view of the general confusion, it has seemed to me worthwhile to review the whole subject, trace the various psychoanalytic ideas about homosexuality, and finally describe the status of the concept today.

148

Freud, in accordance with his libido orientation, considered unconscious homosexuality something basic and causal in neurosis, while more recent analysis has led to the conclusion that homosexuality is but a symptom of more general personal difficulties. Instead of being the basic problem in a given case, it is but one of the manifestations of a character problem, and tends to disappear when the more general character disturbance is resolved.

From Freud's point of view, unconscious homosexuality is to be found in everyone. It is part of the original libido endowment. According to him, it may exist in three different forms. There is latent homosexuality, repressed homosexuality, and overt homosexuality. Latent homosexuality apparently exists in everyone, although perhaps the amount varies from one individual to another. It is not necessarily pathological. Freud assumes it may either find expression in pathological difficulties or in sublimation. Psychoanalysis has to deal with homosexuality as a problem only in its repressed or overt forms. If the use of the term were limited to these two forms, there would be less confusion, although even here Freud speaks of repressed homosexual trends in situations where the sexual content in the usual limited sense of the term does not exist, Freud's view of the matter is based on his concept of bisexuality. According to him part of the original libido endowment is allocated to homosexuality. This libido apparently cannot be converted into heterosexual libido. The two remain distinct and are a part of the original bisexuality. In the course of development one of the two wins out and the loser either becomes sublimated or is the foundation for the formation of neurotic difficulties, so in Freud's theory unconscious homosexuality is an important ingredient of basic personality structure. It has never been clear to me under what conditions Freud thought these unconscious tendencies became conscious or overt. One confusion in the literature arises from the fact that cases are sometimes reported as examples of homosexuality where no clear-cut sexual relation existed, but only a strong neurotic dependency on a member of one's own sex was demonstrated. We are left to assume there is a difference in the dynamics of such a case and one with definite overt manifestations. As far as I know, there has been no analytic data in the classical school on what produces the final violation of cultural taboo—when the individual accepts an overt homosexual way of life—except the very general idea that such a person has a weak superego.

If we question Freud's basic theory of personality, i.e., that the character structure is the result of the sublimation of sexual drives, we have to approach the problem of repressed and overt homosexuality differently. When we discard the libido formula, it is much easier to see that homosexuality is not a clinical entity. There is no clear-cut situation in which it invariably occurs. It appears as a symptom in people of diverse types of character structure. The simple division into active and passive types does not cover the picture, nor are these distinctions always clear-cut. For example, the same individual may be active with a younger partner and passive with an older one. The personality type who happens to have made an overt homosexual adjustment in one case may be almost identical with the personality type who under very similar circumstances makes a heterosexual choice in another case. [Bernard] Robbins describes the sadomasochistic personality as one frequently found among homosexuals. However, as we well know, sadomasochistic heterosexual situations are also very frequent, so the specific choice of the sex object is not explained by his work. We can agree with Freud that all people are bisexual in the sense that they are biologically capable of being sexually roused by either sex, or in fact by a variety of other stimulants. Many people tend to form a more or less lasting attachment to the partner in their sexual pleasure. In childhood, before the taboos of adults are imposed, a state of uncritical enjoyment of body stimulation exists. When the pleasure is shared it may be shared with either sex depending to a great extent on propinquity or availability.

On the basis of the early childhood example it would be interesting to speculate about what might happen if an individual could continue his development in a culture with no sex restrictions. It is possible that most children would eventually develop a preference for the biologically most satisfactory type of sexual gratification and that that would prove to be found in the union of male and female genitals. If it should be found that the heterosexual activity eventually became the preferred form of sex life, would this mean that the other forms had been repressed? If the culture were truly uncritcizing, repression would be unnecessary. Homosexuality would disappear when more satisfactory gratifications were available. It might reappear if the heterosexual possibilities were withdrawn. In other words, it is probable that on the physiological level uninhibited humans would get their sex gratification in any way possible—but if they had a choice they would choose the most pleasurable.

However, most sexual relationships, in addition to the physiological gratification of lust, have meaning also in interpersonal terms. The relationship as a whole has significance. The value of the relationship in turn affects the satisfaction obtained from the sexual activity. Except in some situations to be described presently, where the choice of a homosexual love object is determined by environmental limitations, it would seem that the interpersonal factor, i.e., the type of relationship, the nature of the dependency, the personality of the love object, are all factors which cannot be overlooked in determining whether the choice is a heterosexual or a homosexual way of life. Before discussing this in detail it would be well to look at some of the varying degrees of acceptability of homosexuality in our own society.

We find some form of sexual restriction in most cultures. There is a preferred and acceptable form of sexual behavior while other forms of sexual gratification are in varying degrees of disrepute—some being absolutely forbidden and punishable, some simply being less acceptable. It is obvious that under these circumstances no individual is free to choose. He has to cope with the danger of ostracism if he is driven toward a culturally unacceptable form of sexual behavior. This is definitely one of the problems associated with overt homosexuality in our culture, especially in the case of men. Freud believed one important distinction between a repressed and an overt homosexual was that the former had a stern superego and the latter a weak superego. This is too simple a statement of the problem, for among overt homosexuals we find in addition to the psychopaths who answer to Freud's description, also those who suffer from superegos and are genuinely unhappy about their condition; others who accept their fate with resignation but feel handicapped; some who have lost all sense of self-esteem and think of their sexual behavior as but another evidence of their worthlessness. Also some more fortunate cases through protected circumstances have not happened to come in contact with the more criminal psychopathic elements in homosexual groups, especially in large cities, and due to their isolation or discreet living have not been made acutely aware of society's disapproval. These homosexuals do not feel great conflict about their relationship, although in other respects they are not lacking in a sense of social responsibility, i.e., they do not have weak superegos, to use Freud's term.

Individuals most frequently found in the last named situation are women. This brings us to a consideration of the difference between male and female homosexuality, at least in this culture. Women in general are permitted greater physical intimacy with one another without social disapproval than is the case with men. Kissing and hugging are acceptable forms of friendly expression between women. In America a father is often too self-conscious to kiss his own son, while mother and daughter have no such inhibitions. Ferenczi pointed out that in our culture compulsive heterosexuality is one outgrowth of the taboo on even close friendship with one's own sex. It is obvious that in the case of women there is a much more permissive attitude about friendship with one's own sex and therefore about overt homosexuality. Here until recent times there is a much stronger taboo against obvious nonmarital heterosexual situations. Two overt homosexual women may live together in complete intimacy in many communities without social disapproval if they do not flaunt their inversion by, for example, the assumption of masculine dress or mannerism on the part of one. Sometimes even if they go to this extreme they are thought peculiar rather than taboo. On the other hand, two men attempting the same thing are likely to encounter marked hostility.

Perhaps this difference in the attitude of society has a deep biological origin, to wit: two women may live together in closest intimacy with kisses, caresses, and close bodily contact without overt evidence of sexual gratification; two men in the same situation must know that they are sexually stimulated. Whether this biological factor contributes to the increased tolerance for female homosexuals or not, there are other factors that definitely contribute to making the situation more normal in women. Earlier in the discussion I pointed out that in situations of limited choice an individual makes the best of the sexual partner available. If there is a wide range of choice a person chooses the most desirable. Circumstances producing deprivation—such as any life in remote places—may make strange creatures attractive as sex objects.

However, in general men encounter fewer external causes of deprivation than women. So when a man becomes an overt homosexual it is almost always due to difficulties within himself. Of these society is not tolerant. It tends to label the man as weak. Women are more frequently in an isolated situation with regard to heterosexual possibilities than men. Age and physical unattractiveness handicap women more. More conventions surround her search for a partner so that even when young and attractive she may find herself for a long period without socially acceptable means of meeting men. Thus strong external difficulties often lead relatively mature women into homosexual relationships, whereas overt homosexuality in the male is usually an expression of grave personality disorder. I do not wish to imply that there are no severely disturbed homosexual women, but rather that society's tolerance may be due to the greater proportion of fairly healthy homosexual women.

The different cultural attitudes toward the sissy and the tomboy again show society's greater tolerance for the female homosexual type. When a boy is called a sissy he feels stigmatized and the group considers that it has belittled him. No such disapproval goes with a girl's being called a tomboy. In fact she often feels considerable pride in the fact. Probably these names get their value from childhood ideas that courage and daring are desirable traits in both sexes. So the sissy is a coward, a mama's boy, and the tomboy is a brave girl who can hold her own with a boy her size. These attitudes probably became a part of later attitudes toward homosexuality in the two sexes.

The attitude toward homosexuality in Western society may be summed up as follows. In most circles it is looked upon as an unacceptable form of sexual activity. When external circumstances make the attainment of a heterosexual choice temporarily or permanently impossible, as with women, or men in isolated situations, society is more tolerant of the homosexual situations. Also, character traits usually associated with the homosexual affect the degree of disapproval of the individual invert. Thus the tomboy receives less contempt than the sissy. People who for reasons external to their own personality find their choice of love object limited to their own sex may be said to be normal homosexuals, in the sense that they utilize the best type of interpersonal relationship available to them. These people are not the problem of psychopathology.

The question that concerns us as psychotherapists is what kind of inner difficulty predisposes the individual to the choice of overt homosexuality as his preferred form of interpersonal relationship. When no external limitations are in evidence is there any one predisposing factor or may it appear in a variety of interpersonal difficulties? Is it an outgrowth of a definite personality structure or do accidental factors add it to an already burdened personality, or are there in each case definite tendencies from early childhood leading in the direction of homosexuality? It is possible that each of these situations may occur as a predisposing background, and that in each case the meaning of the symptom of homosexuality is determined by the background. In other words, homosexuality is not a clinical entity, but a symptom with different meanings in different personality setups. One might compare its place in the neurosis to that of a headache in various diseases. A headache may be the result of brain tumor, a sinus, a beginning infectious disease, a migraine attack, an emotional disturbance, or a blow on the head. When the underlying disease is treated successfully the headache disappears.

Similarly overt homosexuality may express fear of the opposite sex, fear of adult responsibility, a need to defy authority, an attempt to cope with hatred or competitive attitudes to members of one's own sex, or it may represent a flight from reality into absorption in body stimulation very similar to the autoerotic activities of the schizophrenic, or it may be a symptom of destructiveness of oneself or others. These do not exhaust the possibilities of its meaning. They merely represent situations which I have personally found in analyzing cases. The examples indicate the wide scope of difficulties that may find expression in the symptom.

Our next concern is to determine, if possible, why this symptom is chosen as a solution of the difficulty. Can we invariably show in the given individual tendencies which can clearly be traced from childhood predisposing to homosexuality? In many cases this seems to be true. In our culture most children grow up in very close relationship to two individuals of opposite sexes. It is clear that a child has a distinct relationship to each parent, that sexual interest and curiosity plays some part in this, but there are usually more important things. The relationship is to a great extent molded by the role of that parent in the child's life. For example, the mother is usually more closely associated with the bodily needs than is the father. The father's function varies widely. In some families he stands for discipline, in others he is the playmate, in others he shares the care with the mother. These facts influence the child's reaction to the parent. In addition, the child has a relationship to the parent in terms of the kind of person the parent is. He learns early which parent wields the power, which loves him more, which is the more dependable, and which one can be manipulated best by his techniques, etc. Consideration of these facts determine which parent he prefers and where his allegiance lies. A very important determining influence in the development of homosexuality is the child's awareness that his sex was a disappointment to his parents or to the more important parent, especially if their disappointment leads them to treat the child as if he were of the opposite sex. However, none of these considerations invariably produce homosexuality in the adult. Girls who wished to be boys may grow up without any special interest in their own sex. Boys with gentle motherly qualities often marry and find satisfaction in mothering their own children without ever having gone through a struggle against homosexuality. If their father happened to be the strongest, most loving and constructive influence in a boy's life, and the mother failed him badly, the boy may become a homosexual, but it is equally probable that he will seek a woman of his father's personality type, or if he is more seriously damaged he will be driven to marry a woman with a destructive influence on him somewhat in the pattern of his mother, or he may even become involved in a homosexual relation with a destructive man. We can in the same manner take up all the possible personality combinations found in parents and show that they in themselves do not predetermine the choice of the sex of the later partner.

Sexual relationships seem to be determined along two main lines. There is the constructive choice, where mutual helpfulness and affection dominate the picture, and there is the destructive choice, where the individual finds himself bound to the person he fears and who may destroy him—the moth and flame fascination. There are of course many in-between situations where, for example, the partnership is on the whole constructive but has some destructive elements, etc. This distinction cuts across sex lines. We find both types of heterosexual relationships and both types of homosexual ones.

We are therefore in pursuit of definite predetermining factors in the formation of homosexuality. Two other considerations are important in this respect: the degree of personality damage and the role of accidental factors. People who have been greatly intimidated or have a low self-esteem and who therefore have difficulties in making friends and being comfortable with people have a tendency to cling to their own sex because it is less frightening. They feel understood by people like themselves. There is not the terrifying unpredictability of the unknown. Moreover, relationship with the opposite sex makes greater demands—the man is expected to support the woman, a woman is expected to have children. These require a more mature sense of responsibility. Also the frightened woman fears to test whether she is sufficiently attractive to win a man, and the frightened man fears he may not be sufficiently successful to attract a woman. Again, however, these situations do not invariably produce homosexuality, but homosexuality is a partial solution and is at least one step above isolation.

The overt homosexual situation attracts immature or neurotic people of both sexes because it offers an intimacy with relative freedom from social responsibility. There are no children as a result of this union. No law will force a person unwillingly to support a mate. It also attracts people who have difficulties in forming intimate attachments in general. As already mentioned, one's own sex is less frightening because it is familiar. The relationship looks less permanent, less entrapping, as if one could get away at any time. To be sure, the appearance of freedom often proves deceptive, for neurotic attachments with either sex have a way of becoming binding through neurotic dependencies. Among men the fear of the struggle for existence tempts a certain number to become dependent financially as well as otherwise on another man.

Thus far we have shown that various personality problems may find partial solution in a homosexual symptom, but we have found nothing that specifically produces homosexuality. Great stress has been laid on the importance of early seduction by homosexuals, and many homosexuals attribute their way of life to such experiences. However, many people have such experiences without becoming homosexual. It is probable that a homosexual experience to a boy already heavily burdened, fearing women, and feeling unequal to life may add the decisive last touch to his choice of neurosis, while a similar seduction of a boy not afraid of life is but an incident in the process of investigation of life, and he simply goes on to master new experiences. We know that homosexual play is very frequent in preadolescence and causes no serious disturbance in the majority of children.

Perhaps because of Freud's great emphasis on the sexual origin of neurosis and perhaps also because of the strong cultural disapproval we are likely to think of homosexuality as a more important symptom than it really is. It seems certain from analysis in recent years that it is a problem that tends to disappear when the general character problems are solved. Even as a symptom, homosexuality does not present a uniform appearance. There are as many different types of homosexual behavior as of heterosexual, and the interpersonal relations of homosexuals present the same problems as are found in heterosexual situations. So we find the mother-child attachment sometimes the important part in the picture. Frequently competitive and sadomasochistic feelings dominate the union. Relationships based on hatred and fear and relationships of mutual helpfulness exist. Promiscuity is possibly more frequent among homosexuals than heterosexuals, but its significance in the personality structure is very similar in the two. In both the chief interest is in genitals and body stimulation. The individual chosen to share the experience is not important. The sexual activity is compulsive and is the sole interest. In fact in much activity carried on in movies, the partner is not even clearly seen and often not a word is exchanged.

At the other extreme is the homosexual marriage, by which I mean a relatively durable, long-term relationship between two people in which the interests and personalities of each are important to the other. Here again we may find all of the pictures of a neurotic heterosexual marriage, the same possessiveness, jealousies, and struggles for power. The idea may be at least theoretically entertained that a homosexual adult love relationship can exist. Adult love seems to be a rare experience in our culture anyway and would doubtless be even more rare among homosexuals because a person with the necessary degree of maturity would probably prefer a heterosexual relation unless external circumstances in his life made this impossible.

So the actual choice of homosexuality as the preferred form of interpersonal relations may have different origins in different cases, as I have indicated. If it is due to some one specific situation or combination of circumstances, that has not yet been discovered.

If we cannot find a specific cause, can we find specific needs which it satisfies? Obviously it gives sexual satisfaction, and for a person unable to make contact with the opposite sex, this is important. Also, because it requires a partner it helps a person cope with the problems of loneliness and isolation. The very fact of belonging to a culturally taboo group has its satisfactions. One can feel defiant, brave, strong, and as a member of a band against the world the feeling of ostracism is lessened. We have spoken earlier of other satisfactions, such as freedom from responsibility, and financial support, especially in the case of some male homosexuals.

An overt homosexual way of life can play a constructive or destructive role in the personality. It may be the best type of human relation of which the individual is capable and as such is better than isolation. This would apply especially to the mother-child type of dependencies found in homosexuals of both sexes. Or it may be an added destructive touch in a deteriorating personality. In no case will it be found to be the cause of the rest of the neurotic structure, the basic origin of the neurosis, although after it is established it may add its contribution to the problems. As in the case of other symptoms in neurosis, psychoanalysis must deal primarily with the personality structure, realizing that the symptom is a secondary development from that.

# IV

Social Character and Love

# 10

## Selfishness and Self-Love (1939)

Modern culture is pervaded by a taboo on selfishness. It teaches that to be selfish is sinful and that to love others is virtuous. To be sure, this doctrine is not only in flagrant contradiction to the practices of modern society but it also is in opposition to another set of doctrines which assumes that the most powerful and legitimate drive in man is selfishness and that each individual by following this imperative drive also does the most for the common good. The existence of this latter type of ideology does not affect the weight of the doctrines which declare that selfishness is the arch evil and love for others the main virtue. Selfishness, as it is commonly used in these ideologies, is more or less synonymous with self-love. The alternatives are either to love others, which is a virtue, or to love oneself, which is a sin.

This principle has found its classic expression in Calvin's theology. Man is essentially bad and powerless. He can do nothing—absolutely nothing—good on the basis of his own strength or merits. "We are not our own," says Calvin in his

163

*Institutes of the Christian Religion* (Calvin 1928, Book 3, 619), "therefore neither our reason nor our will should predominate in our deliberations and actions. We are not our own; therefore, let us not propose it as our end, to seek what may be expedient for us according to the flesh. We are not our own; therefore, let us, as far as possible, forget ourselves and all things that are ours. On the contrary, we are God's; to him, therefore, let us live and die. For, as it is the most devastating pestilence which ruins people if they obey themselves, it is the only haven of salvation not to know or to want anything by oneself but to be guided by God who walks before us."

Man should not only have the conviction of his absolute nothingness. He should do everything to humiliate himself. "For I do not call it humility," says Calvin (*Ibid.*, 681), "if you suppose that we have anything left . . . we cannot think of ourselves as we ought to think without utterly despising everything that may be supposed an excellence in us. This humility is unfeigned submission of a mind overwhelmed with a weighty sense of its own misery and poverty; for such is the uniform description of it in the word of God."

This emphasis on the nothingness and wickedness of the individual implies that there is nothing he should like about himself. This doctrine is rooted in contempt and hatred for oneself. Calvin makes this point very clear; he speaks of "self-love" as of a "pest" (*Ibid.*, 622).

If the individual finds something in himself "on the strength of which he finds pleasure in himself," he betrays this sinful self-love. This fondness for himself will make him sit in judgment over others and despise them. Therefore, to be fond of oneself, to like anything about oneself is one of the greatest imaginable sins. It excludes love for others and is identical with selfishness.

There are fundamental differences between Calvin's theology and Kant's philosophy, yet the basic attitude toward the problem of love for oneself has remained the same. According to Kant, it is a virtue to want the happiness of others, while to want one's own happiness is ethically "indifferent," since it is something which the nature of man is striving for and a natural striving cannot have positive ethical sense. (Cf. Kant 1909, esp. Part I, 126) Kant admits that one must not give up one's claims for happiness; under certain circumstances it can even be a duty to be concerned with one's happiness; partly because health, wealth, and the like, can be means which are necessary to fulfill one's duty, partly because the lack of happiness—poverty—can seduce a person from fulfilling his duty. (*Ibid.*, Part I, 186) But love for oneself, striving for one's own happiness, can never be a virtue. As an ethical principle, the striving for one's own happiness "is the most objectionable one, not merely because it is false, . . . but because the springs it provides for morality are such as rather undermine it and destroy its sublimity. . . ." (*Ibid.*—in particular *Fundamental Principles of the Metaphysics of Morals*; second section, 61) Kant differentiates in egotism, self-love, philautia—a benevolence for oneself; and arrogance—the pleasure in oneself. "Rational self-love" must be restricted by ethical principles, the pleasure in oneself must be battered down, and the individual must come to feel humiliated in comparing himself with the sanctity of moral laws. (*Ibid.*, Part I, 165) The individual should find supreme happiness in the fulfillment of his duty. The realization of the moral principle—and, therefore, of the individual's happiness—is only possible in the general whole, the nation, the state. Yet, "the welfare of the state—*salus rei publicae suprema lex est*—is not identical with the welfare of the citizens and their happiness."

In spite of the fact that Kant shows a greater respect for the integrity of the individual than did Calvin or Luther, he states that even under the most tyrannical government the individual has no right to rebel and must be punished no less than with death if he threatens the sovereign. (Kant 1907, 126) Kant emphasizes the native propensity for evil in the nature of man (Kant 1934, esp. Book I), for the suppression of which the moral law, the categorical imperative, is necessary unless man should become a beast and human society should end in wild anarchy.

In discussing Calvin's and Kant's systems, their emphasis on the nothingness of man has been stressed. Yet, as already suggested, they also emphasize the autonomy and dignity of the individual, and this contradiction runs through their writings. In the philosophy of the enlightenment period the individual's claims and happiness have been emphasized much more strongly by others than by Kant, for instance by Helvetius. This trend in modern philosophy has found an extreme expression by Stirner and Nietzsche. In the way that they often phrase the problem—though not necessarily in their real meaning—they share one basic premise of Calvin and Kant: that love for others and love for oneself are alternatives. But in contradiction to those authors, they denounce love for others as weakness and self-sacrifice and postulate egotism, selfishness, and self-love—they too confuse the issue by not clearly differentiating between these phenomena—as virtue. Thus Stirner says: "Here, egoism, selfishness must decide, not the principle of love, not love motives like mercy, gentleness, good-nature, or even justice and equity—for iustitia too is a phenomenon of love, a product of love: love knows only sacrifice and demands self-sacrifice." (Stirner 1912, 339)

The kind of love denounced by Stirner is the masochistic dependence that makes the individual a means for achieving the purposes of somebody or something outside himself. With this conception of love could he scarcely avoid a formulation which postulated ruthless egotism as a goal. The formulation is, therefore, highly polemical and overstates the point. The positive principle with which Stirner was concerned was directed against an attitude which had run through Christian theology for many centuries—and which was vivid in the German idealism which was passing in his time; namely, to bend the individual to submit to and find his center in a power and a principle outside of himself. To be sure, Stirner was not a philosopher of the stature of Kant or Hegel, yet he had the courage to make a radical rebellion against that side of idealistic philosophy which negated the concrete individual and thus helped the absolute state to retain its oppressive power over the individual. Although there is no comparison between the depth and scope of the two philosophers, Nietzsche's attitude in many respects is similar to that of Stirner. Nietzsche also denounces love and altruism as the expressions of weakness and self-negation. For Nietzsche, the quest for love is typical of slaves who cannot fight for what they want and, therefore, try to get it through "love." Altruism and love for mankind is thus a sign of degeneration. (Cf. Nietzsche 1910, in particular stanzas 246, 362, 369, 373 and 728) For him, it is the essence of a good and healthy aristocracy that is ready to sacrifice countless people for its interests without having a guilty conscience. Society should be a "foundation and scaffolding by means of which a select class of beings may be able to elevate themselves to their higher duties, and in general to their higher existence." (Nietzsche 1907, 225) Many quotations could be added to document this spirit of sadism, contempt, and brutal egotism. This side of Nietzsche has often been understood as the philosophy of Nietzsche. Is this true; is this the "real" Nietzsche?

To answer this question would require a detailed analysis of his work which cannot be attempted here. There are various reasons which made Nietzsche express himself in the sense mentioned above. First of all, as in the case of Stirner, his philosophy is a reaction—a rebellion—against the philosophical tradition of subordinating the empirical individual to a power and a principle outside of himself. His tendency to over-statements shows this reactive quality. Second, there were traits in Nietzsche's personality, a tremendous insecurity and anxiety, which explain that, and why he had sadistic impulses which led him to those formulations. Yet, these trends in Nietzsche do not seem to me to be the "essence" of his personality nor the corresponding views the essence of his philosophy. Finally Nietzsche shared some of the naturalistic ideas of his time as they were expressed in the materialistic-biologistic philosophy, for which the concepts of the physiological roots of psychic phenomena and the "survival of the fittest" were characteristic. This interpretation does not do away with the fact that Nietzsche shared the view that there is a contradiction between love for others and love for oneself. Yet it is important to notice that Nietzsche's views contain the nucleus from development of which this wrong dichotomy can be overcome. The "love" which he attacks is one which is rooted not in one's own strength, but in one's own weakness. "Your neighbor love is your bad love for yourselves. You flee into your neighbor from yourselves and would fain make a virtue thereof. But I fathom your 'unselfishness.' " He states explicitly, "You cannot stand yourselves and you do not love yourselves sufficiently." (Nietzsche, s. a., 75) The individual has for Nietzsche "an enormously great significance" (Nietzsche 1910, stanza 785). The "strong" individual is the one who has "true kindness, nobility, greatness of soul, which does not give in order to take, which does not want to excel by being kind;—'waste' as type of true kindness, wealth of the person as a premise." (*Ibid.*, stanza 935)

He expresses the same thought also in *Thus Spake Zarathu-*

*stra*: "The one goeth to his neighbor because he seeketh himself, the other one because would he fain lose himself." (Nietzsche, s. a., 76)

The essence of these views is: love is a phenomenon of abundance, its premise is the strength of the individual who can give. Love is affirmation, "it seeketh to create what is loved!" (*Ibid.*, 102) To love another person is only a virtue if it springs from this inner strength, but it is detestable if it is the expression of the basic inability to be oneself. (Cf. Nietzsche 1910, stanza 820; Nietzsche 1911, stanza 35; Nietzsche 1991a stanza 2; Nietzsche, *Nachlaß*, 63–64)

However, the fact remains that Nietzsche left the problem of the relationship between self-love and love for others as unsolved antinomy, even if by interpreting him one may surmise in what direction his solution would have been found. (Compare the important paper by Max Horkheimer [1936], which deals with the problem of egotism in modern history.)

The doctrine that selfishness is the arch evil that one has to avoid and that to love oneself excludes loving others is by no means restricted to theology and philosophy. It is one of the stock patterns used currently in home, school, church, movies, literature, and all the other instruments of social suggestion. "Don't be selfish" is a sentence which has been impressed upon millions of children, generation after generation. It is hard to define what exactly it means. Consciously, most parents connect with it the meaning not to be egotistical, inconsiderate, without concern for others. Factually, they generally mean more than that. "Not to be selfish" implies not to do what one wishes, to give up one's own wishes for the sake of those in authority, i.e., the parents, and later the authorities of society. "Don't be selfish," in the last analysis, has the same ambiguity that we have seen in Calvinism. Aside from its obvious implication, it means, "don't love yourself," "don't be yourself," but submit your life to something more important than yourself, be it an outside power or the internalization of that power as "duty." "Don't be selfish" becomes one of the most powerful ideological weapons in suppressing spontaneity and the free development of personality. Under the pressure of this slogan one is asked for every sacrifice and for complete submission: only those aims are "unselfish" which do not serve the individual for his own sake but for the sake of somebody or something outside of him.

This picture, we must repeat, is in a certain sense one-sided. Beside the doctrine that one should not be selfish, the opposite doctrine is propagandized in modern society: have your own advantage in mind, act according to what is best for you—and by doing so, you will also bring about the greatest advantage for all others. As a matter of fact, the idea that the pursuit of individual egotism is the basis for the development of general welfare is the principle on which competitive capitalism has been built. It may seem strange that two such seemingly contradictory principles could be taught side by side in one culture. Of the fact, there can be no doubt. One result of this contradiction of ideological patterns certainly is confusion in the individual. To be torn between the one and the other doctrine is a serious blockage in the process of integration of personality and has often led to neurotic character formation. (This point has been emphasized by Horney [1937] and by Lynd [1939].)

One must observe that this contradictory pair of doctrines has had an important social function. The doctrine that everybody should pursue his individual advantage obviously was a necessary stimulus for private initiative on which the modern economic structure is built. The social function of the doctrine "don't be selfish" was an ambiguous one. For the broad masses of those who had to live on the level of mere subsistence, it was an important aid to resignation to having wishes which were unattainable under the given socioeconomic system. It was important that this resignation should be one which was not thought of as being brought about by external pressure, since the inevitable result of such a feeling has to be a more or less conscious grudge and a defiance against society. By making this resignation a moral virtue, such a reaction could to a considerable extent be avoided. While this aspect of the social function of the taboo on selfishness is obvious, another, its effect upon the privileged minority, is somewhat more complicated. It only becomes clear if we consider further the meaning of "selfishness." If it means to be concerned with one's economic advantage, certainly the taboo on selfishness would have been a severe handicap to the economic initiative of businessmen. But what it really meant, especially in the earlier phases of English and American culture was, as has been pointed out before: Don't do what you want, don't enjoy yourself, don't spend money or energy for pleasure, but feel it as your duty to work, to be successful, to be prosperous.

It is the great merit of Max Weber to have shown that this principle of what he calls *innerweltliche Askese* (innerworldly asceticism) was an important condition for creating an attitude in which all energy could be directed toward work and the fulfillment of duty. (Cf. Weber 1930) The tremendous economic achievements of modern society would not have been possible if this kind of asceticism had not absorbed all energy to the purpose of thrift and relentless work. It would transcend the scope of this paper to enter into an analysis of the character structure of modern man as he emerged in the sixteenth century. Suffice it to say here that the economic and social changes in the fifteenth and sixteenth centuries destroyed the feeling of security and "belonging" that was typical of the members of medieval society. The socioeconomic position of the urban middle class, the peasantry, and the nobility were shaken in their foundations (Cf. Pascal 1933; Kraus 1930; Tawney 1926); impoverishment, threats to traditional economic positions as well as new chances for economic success arose. Religious and spiritual ties which had established a rounded and secure world for the individual had been broken. The individual found himself completely alone in the world, paradise was lost for good, his success and failure were decided by the laws of the market; the basic relationship to everyone else had become one of merciless competition. The result of all this was a new feeling of freedom attended, however, by an increased anxiety. This anxiety, in its turn, created a readiness for new submission to religious and secular authorities even more strict than the previous ones had been.

The new individualism on the one hand, anxiety and submission to authority on the other, found their ideological expression in Protestantism and Calvinism. At the same time, these religious doctrines did much to stimulate and increase these new attitudes. But even more important than the submission to external authorities was the fact that the authorities were internalized, that man became the slave of a master inside himself instead of one outside. This internal master drove the individual to relentless work and striving for success and never allowed him to be himself and enjoy himself. There was a spirit of distrust and hostility directed not only against the outside world, but also toward one's own self.

This modern type of man was selfish in a twofold sense: he had little concern for others and he was anxiously concerned with his own advantage. But was this selfishness really a concern for himself as an individual, with all his intellectual and sensual potentialities? Had "he" not become the appendix of his socioeconomic role, a cog in the economic machine, even if sometimes an important cog? Was he not the slave of this machine even if he subjectively felt as if he were following his own orders? Was his selfishness identical with self-love or was it instead rooted in the very lack of it?

We must postpone answering these questions, since we have

still to finish a brief survey of the doctrine of selfishness in modern society. The taboo on selfishness has been reinforced in the authoritarian systems. One of the ideological corner-stones of National-Socialism is the principle: "Public good takes precedence over private good" ("Gemeinnutz geht vor Eigennutz"). According to the original propaganda technique of National-Socialism, the thought was phrased in a form pur-posed to permit the workers to believe in the "Socialist" part of the Nazi program. However, if we consider its meaning in the context of the whole Nazi philosophy, the implication is this: the individual should not want anything for himself; he should find his satisfaction in the elimination of his individu-ality and in participating as a small particle in the greater whole of the race, the state, or its symbol, the leader. While Protestantism and Calvinism emphasized individual liberty and responsibility even as it emphasized the nothingness of the in-dividual, Nazism is focused essentially on the latter. Only the "born" leaders are an exception, and even they should feel themselves as instruments of someone higher up in the hier-archy—the supreme leader as an instrument of destiny.

The doctrine that love for oneself is identical with "selfish-ness," and that it is an alternative to love for others has per-vaded theology, philosophy, and the pattern of daily life; it would be surprising if one would not find the same doctrine also in scientific psychology, but here as an allegedly objective statement of facts. A case in point is Freud's theory on narcis-sism. He says, in short, that man has a certain quantity of libido. Originally, in the infant, all this libido has as its objec-tive the child's own person, primary narcissism. Later on, the libido is directed from one's own person toward other objects. If a person is blocked in his "object-relationships," the libido is withdrawn from the object and returned to one's own per-son, secondary narcissism. According to Freud, there is an al-most mechanical alternative between ego-love and object-love.

The more love I turn toward the outside world the less love I have for myself, and vice versa. Freud is thus moved to describe the phenomenon of falling in love as an impoverishment of one's self-love because all love is turned to an object outside of oneself. Freud's theory of narcissism expresses basically the same idea that runs through Protestant religion, idealistic philosophy, and the everyday patterns of modern culture. This by itself does not indicate that he is right or wrong. Yet, this translation of the general principle into the categories of empirical psychology gives us a good basis for examining the principle.

These questions arise: Does psychological observation support the thesis that there is a basic contradiction and the state of alternation between love for oneself and love for others? Is love for oneself the same phenomenon as selfishness? Is there a difference or are they in fact opposites?

Before we turn to the discussion of the empirical side of the problem, it may be noted that from a philosophical viewpoint, the notion that love for others and love for oneself are contradictory is untenable. If it is a virtue to love my neighbor as a human being, why must not I love myself too? A principle which proclaims love for man but which taboos love for myself, exempts me from all other human beings. The deepest experience of human existence, however, is to have this experience with regard to oneself. There is no solidarity of man in which I myself am not included. A doctrine which proclaims such an exclusion proves its objective insincerity by this very fact.

We have come here to the psychological premises on which the conclusions of this paper are built. Generally, these premises are: not only others, but also we ourselves are the "object" of our feelings and attitudes; the attitude toward others and toward ourselves, far from being contradictory, runs basically parallel. (This viewpoint has been emphasized by Horney

1939, esp. Chapters 5 and 7.) With regard to the problem under discussion this means: Love for others and love for ourselves are not alternatives. Neither are hate for others and hate for ourselves alternatives. On the contrary, an attitude of love for themselves will be found in those who are at least capable of loving others. Hatred against oneself is inseparable from hatred against others, even if on the surface the opposite seems to be the case. In other words, love and hatred, in principle, are indivisible as far as the difference between "objects" and one's own self is concerned.

To clarify this thesis, it is necessary to discuss the problem of hatred and love. With regard to hatred one can differentiate between "reactive hatred" and "character-conditioned hatred." By reactive hatred I mean a hatred which is essentially a reaction to an attack on one's life, security, or ideals or on some other person that one loves and identifies oneself with. Its premise is one's positive attitude toward one's life, toward other persons, and toward ideals. If there is a strong affirmation of life, a strong hatred necessarily is aroused if life is attacked. If there is love, hatred must be aroused if the loved one is attacked. There is no passionate striving for anything which does not necessitate hatred if the object of this striving is attacked. Such hatred is the counterpoint of life. It is aroused by a specific situation, its aim is the destruction of the attacker and, in principle, it ends when the attacker is defeated. (Nietzsche 1911a, Stanza 2, has emphasized the creative function of destruction.)

Character-conditioned hatred is different. To be sure, the hatred rooted in the character structure once arose as a reaction to certain experiences undergone by the individual in his childhood. It then became a character trait of the person; he is hostile. His basic hostility is observable even when it is not giving rise to manifest hatred. There is something in the facial expression, gestures, tone of voice, kind of jokes, little unintentional reactions which impress the observer as indications of the fundamental hostility, which also could be described as a continuous readiness to hate. It is the basis from which reactive hatred springs if and when it is aroused by a specific stimulus. This hate reaction can be perfectly rational; as much so, as a matter of fact, as is the case in the situations which were described as arousing reactive hatred. There is, however, a fundamental difference. In the case of reactive hatred it is the situation which creates the hatred. In the case of character-conditioned hatred an "idling" hostility is actualized by the situation. In the case where the basic hatred is aroused, the person involved appears to have something like a feeling of relief, as though he were happy to have found the rational opportunity to express his lingering hostility. He shows a particular kind of satisfaction and pleasure in his hatred which is missing in the case of an essentially reactive hatred.

In the case of a proportionality between hate reaction and external situation, we speak of a "normal" reaction, even if it is the actualization of character-conditioned hatred. From this normal reaction to an "irrational" reaction found in the neurotic or psychotic person, there are innumerable transitions and no sharp demarcation line can be drawn. In the irrational hate reaction, the emotion seems disproportionate to the actual situation. Let me illustrate by referring to a reaction which psychoanalysts have ample opportunity to observe; an analysand has to wait ten minutes because the analyst is delayed. The analysand enters the room, wild with rage at the offense done to him by the analyst. Extreme cases can be observed more clearly in psychotic persons; in those the disproportionality is still more striking. Psychotic hatred will be aroused by something which from the standpoint of reality is not at all offensive. Yet, from the standpoint of his own feeling it is offensive, and thus the irrational reaction is irrational only from the standpoint of external objective reality, not from the subjective premises of the person involved.

The lingering hostility can also be purposely aroused and turned into manifest hatred by social suggestion, that is, propaganda. If such propaganda which wants to instill people with hatred toward certain objects is to be effectual, it must build upon the character-conditioned hostility in the personality structure of the members of the groups to which it appeals. A case in point is the appeal of Nazism to the group which formed its nucleus, the lower middle class. Latent hostility was peculiarly the lot of the members of this group long before it was actualized by Nazi propaganda and that is why they were such fertile soil for this propaganda.

Psychoanalysis offers ample opportunity to observe the conditions responsible for the existence of hatred in the character structure.

The decisive factors for arousing character-conditioned hatred may be stated to be all the different ways by which spontaneity, freedom, emotional and physical expansiveness, and the development of the "self" of the child are blocked or destroyed. The means of doing this are manifold; they vary from open, intimidating hostility and terror, to a subtle and "sweet" kind of "anonymous authority," which does not overtly forbid anything but says: "know you will or will not like this or that."

Simple frustration of instinctual impulses does not create deep-seated hostility; it only creates a reactive hate reaction. Yet, this was Freud's assumption and his concept of the Oedipus complex is based on it; it implies that the frustration of sexual wishes directed toward the father or the mother creates hatred which in its turn leads to anxiety and submission. To be sure, frustration often appears as a symptom of something which does create hostility: not taking the child seriously, blocking his expansiveness, not allowing him to be free. But the real issue is not isolated frustration but the fight of the child against those forces which tend to suppress his freedom and spontaneity. There are many forms in which the fight for freedom is fought and many ways in which the defeat is disguised. The child may be ready to internalize the external authority and be "good," it may overtly rebel and yet remain dependent. It may feel that it "belongs" by completely conforming to the given cultural patterns at the expense of the loss of its individual self—the result is always a lesser or greater degree of inner emptiness, the feeling of nothingness, and anxiety; and resulting from all that a chronic hatred, and ressentiment, which Nietzsche characterized very well as *Lebensneid*, envy of life.

There is a slight difference, however, between hatred and this envy of life. The aim of hatred is in the last analysis the destruction of the object outside of my self. By destroying it I attain strength in relative, although not in absolute terms. In envy of life, the begrudging attitude aims at the destruction of others too; not, however, in order to gain relative strength, but to have the satisfaction that others are being denied the enjoyment of things which—for external or internal reasons—I cannot enjoy myself. It aims at removing the pain, rooted in my own inability for happiness, by having nobody else who by his very existence demonstrates what I am lacking.

In principle, the same factors condition the development of chronic hatred in a group. The difference here as in general between individual psychology and social psychology is only to be found in this: while in individual psychology, we are looking for the individual and accidental conditions which are responsible for those character traits by which one individual varies from other members of his group, in social psychology we are interested in the character structure as far as it is common to and, therefore, typical of the majority of the members of that group. As to the conditions, we are not looking for accidental individual conditions like an overstrict father or the sudden death of a beloved sister, but for those conditions of life which are a common experience for the group as such. This does not mean the one or the other isolated trait in the whole mode of life, but the total structure of basic life experiences as they are essentially conditioned by the socio-economic situation of a particular group. (Cf. Fromm 1932a)

The child is imbued with the "spirit" of a society long before it makes the direct acquaintance with it in school. The parents represent in their own character structure the spirit prevalent in their society and class and transmit this atmosphere to the child from the day of his birth onward. The family thus is the "psychic agency" of society.

The bearing on our problem of the differentiation in hatred will have become clear by now. While in the case of reactive hatred the stimulus which is at the same time the object, constitutes the "cause" for the hatred; in the case of character-conditioned hatred, the basic attitude, the readiness for hatred, exists regardless of an object and before a stimulus makes the chronic hostility turn into manifest hatred. As has been indicated, originally, in childhood, this basic hatred was brought into existence by certain people, but later it has become part of the personality structure and objects play but a secondary role. Therefore, in its case, there is, in principle, no difference between objects outside of myself and my own self. The idling hostility is always there; its outside objects change according to circumstances and it but depends on certain factors whether I myself become one of the objects of my hostility. If one wants to understand why a certain person is hated in one case, why I myself am hated in another case, one has to know the specific factors in the situation which make others or myself the object of manifest hatred. What interests us in this context, however, is the general principle that character-conditioned hatred is something radiating from an individual and like a searchlight focusing sometimes on this and sometimes on that object, among them myself.

The strength of basic hatred is one of the major problems of our culture. In the beginning of this paper, it has been shown how Calvinism and Protestantism pictured man as essentially evil and contemptible. Luther's hatred against the revolting peasants is of extraordinary intensity.

Max Weber has emphasized the distrust for and hostility toward others which runs through the Puritan literature replete with warnings against having any confidence in the help and friendliness of our fellow men. Deep distrust even toward one's closest friend is recommended by Baxter. Th. Adams says: "He—the 'knowing' man—is blind in no man's cause but best sighted in his own. He confines himself to the circle of his own affairs and thrusts not his fingers in needless fires. . . . He sees the falseness of it [the world] and, therefore, learns to trust himself ever, others so far as not to be damaged by their disappointments." (*Work of the Puritan Divines*, quoted in Weber 1930, 222)

Hobbes assumed that man's nature was that of a predatory animal, filled with hostility, set to kill and rob. Only by the consensus of all, submitting to the authority of the state, could peace and order be created. Kant's opinion of man's nature is not too distant from Hobbes, he too thought that man's nature had a fundamental propensity for evil. Among psychologists, chronic hatred as an inherent part of human nature has been a frequent assumption. William James considered it as being so strong that he took for granted that we all feel a natural repulsion against physical contact with other persons. (Cf. James 1893, esp. vol. 2, 348) Freud, in his theory of the death instinct, assumed that for biological reasons, we all are driven by an irresistible force to destroy either others or ourselves.

Although some of the philosophers of the Enlightenment period believed that the nature of man was good and that his hostility was the product of the circumstances under which he lived, the assumption of hostility as an inherent part of man's nature runs through the ideas of representative thinkers of the modern era from Luther up to our days. We need not discuss whether this assumption is tenable. At any rate, the philosophers and psychologists who held this belief were good observers of man within their own culture, even though they made the mistake of believing that modern man in his essence is not a historical product but is as nature made him to be.

While important thinkers clearly saw the strength of hostility in modern man, popular ideologies and the convictions of the average man tend to ignore the phenomenon. Only a relatively small number of people have an awareness of their fundamental dislike of others. Many have only a feeling of just having little interest or feeling for others. The majority are completely unaware of the intensity of the chronic hatred in themselves as well as in others. They have adopted the feeling that they know they are supposed to have: to like people, to find them nice, unless or until they have actually committed an act of aggression. The very indiscriminateness of this "liking people" shows its thinness or rather its compensatory quality a basic lack of fondness.

While the frequency of underlying distrust and dislike for others is known to many observers of our social scene, the dislike for oneself is a less clearly recognized phenomenon. Yet, this self-hatred may be considered rare only so long as we think of cases in which people quite overtly hate or dislike themselves. Mostly, this self-dislike is concealed in various ways. One of the most frequent indirect expressions of self-dislike are the inferiority feelings so widespread in our culture. Consciously, these persons do not feel that they dislike themselves: what they do feel is only that they are inferior to others, that they are stupid, unattractive, or whatever the particular content of the inferiority feelings is.

To be sure, the dynamics of inferiority feelings are complex and there are factors other than the one with which we are dealing. Yet, this factor is never missing and dislike for oneself or at least a lack of fondness for one's own person is always present and is dynamically an important factor.

A still more subtle form of self-dislike is the tendency toward constant self-criticism. These people do not feel inferior but if they make one mistake, discover something in themselves which should not be so, their self-criticism is entirely out of proportion to the significance of the mistake or the shortcoming. They must either be perfect according to their own standards, or at least perfect enough according to the standards of the people around them so that they get affection and approval. If they feel that what they did was perfect or if they succeed in winning other people's approval, they feel at ease. But whenever this is missing they feel overwhelmed by an otherwise repressed inferiority feeling. Here again, the basic lack of fondness for themselves is one source from which the attitude springs. This becomes more evident if we compare this attitude toward oneself with the corresponding one toward others. If, for example, a man who believes that he loves a woman should feel if she makes any mistake that she is no good, or if his feeling about her is entirely dependent on whether others criticize or praise her, we cannot doubt that there is a fundamental lack of love for her. It is the person who hates who seizes every opportunity to criticize another person and who does not miss any blunder.

The most widespread expression of the lack of fondness for oneself, however, is the way in which people treat themselves.

People are their own slave drivers; instead of being the slaves of a master outside of themselves, they have put the master within. This master is harsh and cruel. He does not give them a moment's rest, he forbids them the enjoyment of any pleasure, does not allow them to do what they want. If they do so, they do it furtively and at the expense of a guilty conscience. Even the pursuit of pleasure is as compulsory as is work. It does not lead them away from the continual restlessness that pervades their lives. For the most part, they are not even aware of this. There are some exceptions. Thus, the banker James Stillman, who, when in the prime of life, had attained wealth, prestige and power reached only by but few people said: "I never in my life have done what I wanted and never shall do so." (Cf. Robeson 1927)

The role of "conscience" as the internalization of external authorities and as the bearer of deep-seated hostility against oneself has been seen clearly by Freud in the formulation of his concept of the superego. He assumed that the superego contains a great deal of the basic destructiveness inherent in man and turns it against him in terms of duty and moral obligation. In spite of objections to Freud's superego theory, which cannot be presented here (see my discussion of the superego in Fromm 1936a), Freud undoubtedly has sensed keenly the hostility and cruelty contained in the "conscience" as it was conceived in the modern era.

What holds true of hostility and hatred holds also true of love. Yet, love for others and self-love is by far a more difficult problem to discuss; and this for two reasons. One is the fact that while hatred is a phenomenon to be found everywhere in our society and, therefore, an easy object for empirical observation and analysis, love is a comparatively rare phenomenon, which lends itself to empirical observation only under difficulties; any discussion of love, therefore, implies the danger of being unempirical and merely speculative. The other difficulty is perhaps even greater. There is no word in our language which has been so much misused and prostituted as the word *love*. It has been preached by those who were ready to condone every cruelty if it served their purpose; it has been used as a disguise under which to force people into sacrificing their own happiness, into submitting their whole self to those who profited from this surrender. It has been used as the moral basis for unjustified demands. It has been made so empty that for many people love may mean no more than that two people have lived together for twenty years just without fighting more often than once a week. It is dangerous and somewhat embarrassing to use such a word. Yet a psychologist may not properly succumb to this embarrassment. To preach love is at best bad taste. But to make a cool and critical analysis of the phenomenon of love and to unmask pseudolove—tasks which cannot be separated from each other—is an obligation that the psychologist has no right to avoid.

It goes without saying that this paper will not attempt to give an analysis of love. Even to describe the psychological phenomena which are conventionally covered by the term *love* would require a good part of a book. One must attempt, however, the presentation necessary to the main trend of thought of this paper.

Two phenomena closely connected with each other are frequently presented as love—the masochistic and sadistic love. In the case of masochistic love, one gives up one's self, one's initiative and integrity in order to become submerged entirely in another person who is felt to be stronger. Because of deep anxieties which give rise to the feeling that one cannot stand on one's own feet, one wants to be rid of one's own individual self and to become part of another being, thus becoming secure and finding a center which one misses in oneself. This surrender of one's own self has often been praised as the example of "the great love." It is actually a form of idolatry, and also an annihilation of the self. The fact that it has been conceived as love has made it the more seductive and dangerous.

The sadistic love, on the other hand, springs from the desire to swallow its object, to make him a will-less instrument in one's own hands. This drive is also rooted in a deep anxiety and an inability to stand alone, but instead of finding increased strength by being swallowed, strength and security are found in having a limited power over the other person. The masochistic as well as the sadistic kind of love are expressions of one basic need which springs from a basic inability to be independent. Using a biological term, this basic need may be called a "need for symbiosis." The sadistic love is frequently the kind of love that parents have for their children. Whether the domination is overtly authoritarian or subtly "modern" makes no essential difference. In either case, it tends to undermine the strength of the self of the child and leads in later years to the development in him of the very same symbiotic tendencies. The sadistic love is not infrequent among adults. Often in relationships of long duration, the respective roles are permanent, one partner representing the sadistic, the other one the masochistic pole of the symbiotic relationship. Often the roles change constantly—a continuous struggle for dominance and submission being conceived as love.

It appears from what has been said that love cannot be separated from freedom and independence. In contradiction to the symbiotic pseudolove, the basic premise of love is freedom and equality. Its premise is the strength, independence, integrity of the self, which can stand alone and bear solitude. This premise holds true for the loving as well as for the loved person. Love is a spontaneous act, and spontaneity means—also literally—the ability to act of one's own free volition. If anxiety and weakness of the self makes it impossible for the individual to be rooted in himself, he cannot love.

This fact can be fully understood only if we consider what

love is directed toward. It is the opposite of hatred. Hatred is a passionate wish for destruction; love is a passionate affirmation of its "object." That means that love is not an "affect" but an active striving, the aim of which is the happiness, development, and freedom of its "object." This passionate affirmation is not possible if one's own self is crippled, since genuine affirmation is always rooted in strength. The person whose self is thwarted can only love in an ambivalent way; that is, with the strong part of his self he can love, with the crippled part he must hate.

The term passionate affirmation easily leads to misunderstanding; it does not mean intellectual affirmation in the sense of purely rational judgment. It implies a much deeper affirmation, in which one's personality takes part as a whole: one's intellect, emotion, and senses. One's eyes, ears, and nose are often as good or better organs of affirmation than one's brain. If it is a deep and passionate one, the affirmation is related to the essence of the "object," not merely toward partial qualities. There is no stronger expression of God's love for man in the Old Testament than the saying at the end of each day of creation: "And God saw that it was good."

There is another possible misunderstanding which should particularly be avoided. From what has been said, one might come to the conclusion that every affirmation is love, regardless of the worthiness of the object to be loved. This would mean that love is a purely subjective feeling of affirmation and that the problem of objective values does not enter into it. The question arises: Can one love the evil? We come here to one of the most difficult problems of psychology and philosophy, a discussion of which can scarcely be attempted here. I must repeat, however, that affirmation in the sense here used is not something entirely subjective. Love is affirmation of life, growth, joy, freedom, and by definition, therefore, the evil which is negation, death, compulsion cannot be loved. Certainly, the subjective feeling can be a pleasurable excitement, consciously conceived in the conventional term of love. The person is apt to believe that he loves, but analysis of his mental content reveals a state very different from what I have discussed as love.

Much the same question arises with regard to certain other problems in psychology, for instance, the problem as to whether happiness is an entirely subjective phenomenon or whether it includes an objective factor. Is a person who feels "happy" in dependence and self-surrender happy because he feels to be so, or is happiness always dependent on certain values like freedom and integrity? One has always used the argument that the people concerned are "happy" to justify their suppression. This is a poor defense. Happiness cannot be separated from certain values, and is not simply a subjective feeling of satisfaction. A case in point is masochism. A person can be satisfied with submission, with torture, or even with death, but there is no happiness in submission, torture, or death. Such considerations seem to leave the ground of psychology and to belong to the field of philosophy or religion. I do not believe that this is so. A sufficiently refined psychological analysis, which is aware of the difference in the qualities of feelings according to the underlying personality structure, can show the difference between satisfaction and happiness. Yet, psychology can be aware of these problems only if it does not try to separate itself from the problem of values. And, in the end does not shrink from the question of the goal and purpose of human existence.

Love, like character-conditioned hatred, is rooted in a basic attitude which is constantly present; a readiness to love, a basic sympathy as one might call it. It is started, but not caused, by a particular object. The ability and readiness to love is a character trait just as is the readiness to hate. It is difficult to say what the conditions favoring the development of this basic

187

sympathy are. It seems that there are two main conditions, a positive and a negative one. The positive one is simply to have experienced love from others as a child. While conventionally, parents are supposed to love their children as a matter of course, this is rather the exception than the rule. This positive condition is, therefore, frequently absent. The negative condition is the absence of all those factors, discussed above, which make for the existence of a chronic hatred. The observer of childhood experiences may well doubt that the absence of these conditions is frequent.

From the premise that actual love is rooted in a basic sympathy there follows an important conclusion with regard to the objects of love. The conclusion is, in principle, the same as was stated with regard to the objects of chronic hatred: the objects of love do not have the quality of exclusiveness. To be sure, it is not accidental that a certain person becomes the object of manifest love. The factors conditioning such a specific choice are too numerous and too complex to be discussed here.

The important point, however, is that love for a particular object is only the actualization and concentration of lingering love with regard to one person; it is not, as the idea of romantic love would have it, that there is only the one person in the world whom one could love, that it is the great chance of one's life to find that person, and that love for him or her results in a withdrawal from all others. The kind of love which can only be experienced with regard to one person demonstrates by this very fact that it is not love, but a symbiotic attachment. The basic affirmation contained in love is directed toward the beloved person as an incarnation of essentially human qualities.

Love for one person implies love for man as such. The kind of "division of labor" as William James calls it—namely, to love one's family, but to be without feeling for the "stranger," is a sign of a basic inability to love. Love for man as such is not, as it is frequently supposed to be, an abstraction coming "after" the love for a specific person, or an enlargement of the experience with a specific object; it is its premise, although genetically it is acquired in the contact with concrete individuals.

From this, it follows that my own self, in principle, is as much an object of my love as another person. The affirmation of my own life, happiness, growth, freedom is rooted in the presence of the basic readiness of and ability for such an affirmation. If an individual has this readiness, he has it also toward himself; if he can only love others, he cannot love at all. In one word, love is as indivisible as hatred with regard to its objects.

The principle which has been pointed out here, that hatred and love are actualizations of a constant readiness, holds true for other psychic phenomena. Sensuality, for instance, is not simply a reaction to a stimulus. The sensual or as one may say, the erotic person, has a basically erotic attitude toward the world. This does not mean that he is constantly excited sexually. It means that there is an erotic atmosphere which is actualized by a certain object, but which is there underneath before the stimulus appears. What is meant here is not the physiologically given ability to be sexually excited, but an atmosphere of erotic readiness, which under a magnifying glass could be observed also when the person is not in a state of actual sexual excitement. On the other hand, there are persons in whom this erotic readiness is lacking. In them, sexual excitement is essentially caused by a stimulus operating on the sexual instinct. Their threshold of stimulation can vary between wide limits, but there is a common quality in this type of sexual excitement; namely, its separateness from the whole personality in its intellectual and emotional qualities.

Another illustration of the same principle is the sense of beauty. There is a type of personality who has a readiness to see beauty. Again, that does not mean that he is constantly looking at beautiful pictures, or people, or scenery; yet, when he sees them a continuously present readiness is actualized, and his sense of beauty is not simply aroused by the object. Here, too, a very refined observation shows that this type of person has a different way of looking at the world, even when he looks at objects which do not stimulate an acute perception of beauty. We could give many more examples for the same principle, if space permitted. The principle should already be clear: While many psychological schools have thought of human reactions in terms of stimulus-response, the principle presented here is that character is a structure of numerous readinesses of the kind mentioned, which are constantly present and are actualized but not caused by an outside stimulus. This view is essential for such a dynamic psychology as psychoanalysis is.

Freud assumed that all these readinesses are rooted in biologically given instincts. It is here assumed that although this holds true for some of them, many others have arisen as a reaction to the individual and social experiences of the individual.

One last question remains to be discussed. Granted that love for oneself and for others in principle runs parallel, how do we explain the kind of selfishness which obviously is in contradiction to any genuine concern for others. The selfish person is only interested in himself, wants everything for himself, is unable to give with any pleasure but is only anxious to take; the world outside himself is conceived only from the standpoint of what he can get out of it; he lacks interest in the needs of others, or respect for their dignity and integrity. He sees only himself, judges everyone and everything from the standpoint of its usefulness to him, is basically unable to love. This selfishness can be manifest or disguised by all sorts of unselfish gestures; dynamically it is exactly the same. It seems obvious that with this type of personality there is a contradiction between the enormous concern for oneself and the lack of concern for others. Do we not have the proof here that there exists an alternative between concern for others and concern for oneself? This would certainly be the case if selfishness and self-love were identical. But this assumption is the very fallacy which has led to so many mistaken conclusions with regard to our problem. Selfishness and self-love far from being identical, actually are opposites.

Selfishness is one kind of greediness. (The German word *Selbstsucht* [addiction to self] very adequately expresses this quality common to all *Sucht*.) Like all greediness, it contains an insatiability, as a consequence of which there is never any real satisfaction. Greed is a bottomless pit which exhausts the person in an endless effort to satisfy the need without ever reaching satisfaction. This leads to the crucial point: close observation shows that while the selfish person is always anxiously concerned with himself, he is never satisfied, is always restless, always driven by the fear of not getting enough, of missing something, of being deprived of something. He is filled with burning envy of anyone who might have more. If we observe still closer, especially the unconscious dynamics, we find that this type of person is basically not fond of himself but deeply dislikes himself. The puzzle in this seeming contradiction is easy to solve. The selfishness is rooted in this very lack of fondness for oneself. The person who is not fond of himself, who does not approve of himself, is in a constant anxiety concerning his own self. He has not the inner security which can exist only on the basis of genuine fondness and affirmation. He must be concerned about himself, greedy to get everything for himself, since basically his own self lacks security and satisfaction. The same holds true with the so-called narcissistic person, who is not so much overconcerned with getting things for himself as with admiring himself. While on the surface it seems that these persons are very much in love with themselves, they actually are not fond of themselves, and their narcissism—like selfishness—is an overcompensation for the basic lack of self-love. Freud has pointed out that the narcissistic person has withdrawn his love from others and turned it toward his own person. While the first part of this statement is true, the second one is a fallacy. He neither loves others nor himself.

It is easier to understand this mechanism when we compare it with overconcern and overprotectiveness for others. Whether it is an oversolicitous mother or an overconcerned husband, sufficiently deep observation shows always one fact: While these persons consciously believe that they are particularly fond of the child or husband, there actually is a deep repressed hostility toward the very objects of their concern. They are overconcerned because they have to compensate not only for a lack of fondness but for an actual hostility.

The problem of selfishness has still another aspect. Is not the sacrifice of one's own person the extreme expression of unselfishness, and, on the other hand, could a person who loves himself make that supreme sacrifice? The answer depends entirely on the kind of sacrifice that is meant. There is one sacrifice, as it has been particularly emphasized in recent years by Fascist philosophy. The individual should give himself up for something outside of himself which is greater and more valuable: the Leader, the race. The individual by himself is nothing and by the very act of self-annihilation for the sake of the higher power finds his destiny. In this concept, sacrificing oneself for something or someone greater than oneself is in itself the greatest attainable virtue. If love for oneself as well as for another person means basic affirmation and respect, this concept is in sharp contrast to self-love. But there is another kind of sacrifice: if it should be necessary to give one's life for the preservation of an idea which has become part of oneself or for a person whom one loves, the sacrifice may be the extreme expression of self-affirmation. Not, of course, an affirmation of one's physical self, but of the self in the sense of the kernel of one's total personality. In this case the sacrifice in itself is not the goal; it is the price to be paid for the realization and affirmation of one's own self. While in this latter case, the sacrifice is rooted in self-affirmation, in the case of what one might call the masochistic sacrifice, it is rooted in the lack of self-love and self-respect; it is essentially nihilistic.

The problem of selfishness has a particular bearing on psychotherapy. The neurotic individual often is selfish in the sense that he is blocked in his relationship to others or overanxious about himself. This is to be expected since to be neurotic means that the integration of a strong self has not been achieved successfully. To be normal certainly does not mean that it has. It means, for the majority of well-adapted individuals, that they have lost their own self at an early age and replaced it completely by a social self offered to them by society. They have no neurotic conflicts because they themselves, and, therefore, the discrepancy between their selves and the outside world, have disappeared. Often the neurotic person is particularly unselfish, lacking in self-assertion and blocked in following his own aims. The reason for this unselfishness is essentially the same as for the selfishness. What he is practically always lacking is self-love. This is what he needs to become well. If the neurotic becomes well, he does not become normal in the sense of the conforming social self. He succeeds in realizing his self, which never had been completely lost and for the preservation of which he was struggling by his neurotic symptoms. A theory, therefore, as Freud's on narcissism which rationalizes the cultural pattern of denouncing self-love by identifying it with selfishness, can have but devastating effects therapeutically. It increases the taboo on self-love. Its effects can only be called positive if the aim of psychotherapy is not to help the individual to be himself; that is, free, spontaneous

and creative—qualities conventionally reserved for artists—
but to give up the fight for his self and conform to the cultural
pattern peacefully and without the noise of a neurosis.

In the present era, the tendency to make of the individual a
powerless atom is increasing. The authoritarian systems tend
to reduce the individual to a will-less and feelingless instrument
in the hands of those who hold the reins; they batter him down
by terror, cynicism, the power of the state, large demonstra-
tions, fierce orators, and all other means of suggestion. When
finally he feels too weak to stand alone, they offer him satisfaction by letting him participate in the strength and glory of
the greater whole, whose powerless part he is. The authoritarian propaganda uses the argument that the individual of the
democratic state is selfish and that he should become unselfish
and socially minded. This is a lie. Nazism substituted the most
brutal selfishness of the leading bureaucracy and of the state
for the selfishness of the average man. The appeal for unselfishness is the weapon to make the average individual still
more ready to submit or to renounce.

The criticism of democratic society should not be that people
are too selfish; this is true but it is only a consequence of something else. What democracy has not succeeded in is to make
the individual love himself; that is, to have a deep sense of
affirmation for his individual self, with all his intellectual, emotional, and sensual potentialities. A puritan-protestant inheritance of self-denial, the necessity of subordinating the
individual to the demands of production and profit, have made
for conditions from which Fascism could spring. The readiness
for submission, the pervert courage which is attracted by the
image of war and self-annihilation, is only possible on the basis
of a—largely unconscious—desperation, stifled by martial
songs and shouts for the Führer. The individual who has
ceased to love himself is ready to die as well as to kill. The
problem of our culture, if it is not to become a Fascist one, is

not that there is too much selfishness but that there is no self-love. The aim must be to create those conditions which make it possible for the individual to realize his freedom, not only in a formal sense, but by asserting his total personality in his intellectual, emotional, sensual qualities. This freedom is not the rule of one part of the personality over another part—conscience over nature, superego over id—but the integration of the whole personality and the factual expression of all the potentialities of this integrated personality.

# 11

## Do We Still Love Life? (1967)

To some of you this question, whether we still love life, may be puzzling, or it may even sound senseless. Do we not all love life? Is this love of life not the ground from which all our activities spring? Could we even stay alive, unless we loved life or made the many efforts to sustain and to improve it? Perhaps you who think this, and the writer who poses the question, can get to understand each other without great difficulty if we try to.

With others this understanding will be more difficult. I am thinking of those of you who react to my question with a certain indignation. I can hear the indignant responses: "How can you dare to doubt that we love life? Our whole civilization, our way of life, our religious feeling, our political ideas,— they all are rooted in this love of life, and your question seems to put in doubt the very fundaments of our culture!" This indignation makes understanding more difficult, as indignation always does, because of its very nature of being a blending between anger and self-righteousness. The angry person can be

196

much more easily reached by words of reason or kindness than the indignant one who protects his anger with the conviction of his own virtuousness. But perhaps even some of those who read the question in the title with indignation might be more ready to listen when they notice that I am not attacking anyone, but that I try to make explicit a danger which only by being made explicit can be overcome.

Indeed, without a certain minimum of love for life, neither an individual nor a culture could exist. We see that some individuals who have lost this minimum love for life become insane, commit suicide, become hopeless alcoholic or drug addicts; we also know that whole societies have been so emptied of love of life and filled with destructiveness that they crumbled and perished, or almost perished. Think of the Aztecs, whose power vanished like dust before a small group of Spaniards; or think of Nazi Germany, which would have committed mass suicide if Hitler's will had prevailed. Thus far we in the Western world are not crumbling, but there are symptoms indicating that it could happen. If we speak of love of life we must first try to understand one another better about the concept of life. It may seem simple to you. You will say life is the opposite of death. The person or animal that is alive can move by himself, and react to stimuli; the dead organism can do nothing of the kind, and in addition it decays and cannot preserve itself, as a stone or a piece of wood can. True enough, that is an elementary way to define life; however, we might try to describe the quality of life a little further. Life always tends to unite and integrate; in other words, life by necessity is a process of constant growth and change. Indeed, when growth and change cease, there is death. Life does not grow wild and unstructured; every living being has its own form and structure implanted in its chromosomes. It can grow more fully, more perfectly, but it cannot grow into what it was not born to become.

Life is always a process; a process of changing and unfolding; a process also of constant interaction between the constitutional structure and the environment into which it was been born. An apple tree can never become a cherry tree; but each can become a more or less beautiful tree, depending on their constitutional endowment and on the environment in which it lives. The degree of moisture and sun that may be a blessing to one plant will be a curse for another. It is not different with man; but unfortunately most parents and teacher know less about humans than a good gardener knows about plants.

To say that life grows according to a structural pattern, and not wildly and unpredictably, does not mean, however—except in a broad sense—that the very individual aspects of a living being are predictable. This is one of the great paradoxes of all life. It is predictable—yet it is not. We know more or less, in a broad outline, what any living being is to become; yet life is full of surprises, it is disorderly compared with the order that nonliving matter presents. If one is so filled with expectations of "order"—which is, after all, a category of his own mind—that he expects "order" in a living being, he will be disappointed. If his desire for order is very strong, he may try to force life into orderly patterns to control it, and in his frustration and fury when he finds out that it cannot be controlled, he may eventually try to strangle and kill it. He has become a hater of life because he could not free himself from the compulsion to control. He has failed in his love for life because, as a French song puts it, "love is the child of liberty."

It should be added that this holds true not only in our attitude toward the life of others, but also toward the life within ourselves. We all know the person who can never be spontaneous, who can never feel free, because he insists on controlling his feelings, thoughts, and actions; he can never act unless he knows precisely what the result will be; he cannot stand any doubt; he frantically seeks certainty, often to be tormented by more doubt when this certainty cannot be found. Such people who are obsessed with the need to control may be kind or cruel, but one condition must be fulfilled: the subject of their interest must be controllable. When this need for control reaches a certain point, the psychiatrist says that such a person suffers from an obsessive-compulsive neurosis and a good deal of sadism. This is a good way of expressing it if one is dealing with the classifications of mental illnesses. From a slightly different viewpoint, however, one might say that this person is suffering from his inability to love life, that he is afraid of life, just as he is afraid of everything that he cannot control.

And this brings us to a principle inherent in love, whether it is love for life or love for a person, an animal, a flower. I can love only when my love is adequate and corresponds to the needs and the nature of that which is loved. If a plant needs little moisture, my love is expressed by letting it have the moisture it needs. If I have preconceived ideas of "what is good for the plant"—for instance, the idea that lots of water is good for everything—I will cripple or kill the plant, because I was not capable of loving it in the way it needed to be loved. It is simply not enough "to love"; it is not enough "to want the best" for another living being; unless I know the need of the plant, the animal, the child, the man or woman, and unless I can let go of my concept of "what is best," of my wish to control, my love becomes destructive, a kiss of death.

Many people cannot understand why, in spite of loving another person deeply or even passionately, they fail to keep his or her love or even drive him away. They complain about the cruelty of their fate, and they cannot understand why their love fails to evoke love in the other person. If they can stop feeling sorry for themselves and blaming life, it would help them, and it might even change the tragic course of events if they would ask themselves whether their love corresponds to the needs of the loved person or whether it is a result of their own fixed ideas about "what is best."

There is only a small step from controlling to using force. What holds true of the former is equally true of the latter; love and force are irreconcilable contradictions, and perhaps there is no more fundamental polarity in human behavior than that between love and force. Both are deeply rooted in our nature; they are the basic possibilities of approaching the world and coping with it. If I speak of force you must not think immediately of violence, aggression, assault, war. These are drastic symptoms of force, but they are not the same as the principle of force. To most people the principle of force appears so natural and self-evident that they do not even recognize that it is a particular principle and not just part of "human nature." The principle of force often appears to be the most adequate and simple solution of a problem.

Think of a mother whose child refuses to do what is necessary. What gets better and quicker results than to force Johnny? You have the power; he must give in—why not use it? Of course, there are many ways of making use of your force, some friendlier and some nastier ones. You can begin by persuading him and not even mentioning the threat of force, which you keep only as your last resource. Or you can threaten immediately. You can use force moderately and only to the extent to which the purpose requires it; or you can, if you are sadistically inclined, use force immediately and far beyond the needs of a situation. Force is not necessarily a physical threat; it can be psychological, using the child's suggestibility or ignorance to deceive him, lie to him, brain-wash him. Force is effective not only as far as a certain aim is concerned; provided your opponent cannot effectively defend himself, it is also a source of great satisfaction for the one who uses it. It seems to prove his strength, his superiority, his potency. Yet how deceptive is this proof! Just because he is bigger and stronger than the child he is superior, while toward a person with a pistol he, this strong man, would be like a child.

The attitude toward children is only one of the manifestations of force. In adult life, individually and socially, it is applied to the same degree, and even a larger degree, since the feelings of tenderness most of us have for children are less likely to soften our attitude toward people our own age, especially strangers. In most interpersonal relationships it is the law that mitigates the use of force. There are many instances in which the law inhibits my use of force as a means of getting another person to act according to my will. But the law represents only the very minimum of protection against force. In most personal relationships it does not effectively intervene. The father who prevents his adolescent son from choosing the career he wants by stopping his allowance; the mother who uses tears and appeals to the son's generosity to dissuade him from marrying the girl of his choice are using force; the employer who threatens to fire a man; the teacher who insists that his students accept his views and gives them poor marks if they fail to do so—all are using force, aware of it or not.

When it comes to the relations between nations, there is no supranational law that mitigates force. The principle of sovereignty, accepted by all nations, says that the state has the right to pursue its interests by all means it considers fit, including, of course—and most important—the force of arms or economic force. We easily persuade ourselves that our use of force is justified defense, yet we are not disturbed by the fact that, in order to attain our own aims, we do not accept any limits to our inflicting death and destruction. We have become so desensitized that we enjoy our breakfast while reading newspaper accounts of men, women, and children being killed or maimed.

The use of force is, of course, rational only if I have more force than my opponent. Hence the logical consequence is the tendency to increase my force and to prevent anyone else, as far as possible, from attaining my level. History, however, shows, better than individual life, that all efforts to secure permanent superiority through the use of force invariably fail. What in the flush of victory seems to be the foundation for centuries of unchanged stability, based on superior force, invariably crumbles after a few decades before the assault of new force or inner devitalization. Hitler's Thousand-Year Reich that lasted only fifteen years is not untypical of triumphs based mainly on force.

Indeed, even when force seemingly brings about the desired results, it has what we would call in a drug "dangerous side effects." On a national scale, it leaves a passionate desire in the injured to retaliate, and at the same time it gives them the moral justification for their own use of force when circumstances permit.

Equally dangerous is the side effect that force has on the people who use it. The user soon begins to confuse the strength of his means of force (wealth, position, prestige, tanks and bombs) with the strength of his own person. In fact, he does not try to make himself stronger, his mind, his love, his aliveness; but he puts all his energies into the attempt to make his means stronger. He becomes impoverished while his force capacity increases; after he arrives at a point of no return, he can do nothing but continue to deal with the world by force and stake everything on his success with his method. He has become less alive, less interested and interesting, more feared and by many, of course, more admired.

The approach of love is the opposite of the approach by force. Love tries to understand, to convince, to stimulate. In doing so, the loving person constantly transforms himself. He becomes more sensitive, more observing, more productive, more himself. Love is not sentimentality or weakness. It is the method of influencing and changing that does not have the dangerous side effects of forcing. Unlike force, it requires patience, inner effort and, most of all, courage. To choose to solve a problem by love requires the courage to stand frustration, to remain patient in spite of setbacks. It requires faith in one's potency, rather than in its perverted facsimile: force.

Have I written anything which you do not know? I do not think so; yet there is good reason for writing it; because while you know it, at the same time you do not. The purpose of my writing about force and love as the two global attitudes toward life is to stimulate you to be aware of what you know and yet are not aware of. Watch your reaction toward your child, a dog, a neighbor, a salesman, a political antagonist, not to speak of a political enemy. How your reflexes become tensed when your will is frustrated; how you look immediately for a means of force; how you feel defeated when you can find none or have none. How often you feel like the Queen in Alice in Wonderland: "Off with the head." Sometimes you must observe very carefully and learn to listen to reactions which are hardly in your consciousness, if you want to recognize your addiction to the shortcut of the use force.

Then try to turn about and renounce the attitude of force. Be alive, patient, stop being concerned only with results, but more and more with the process, and observe how you relax, lose your tenseness and your anxiety. The use of force is one way of solving the problem of human existence. It is a possible way only for those who dispose of the means of force against those whose force is inferior. But while it is a possible way of solving the problem of life, it is not a satisfactory one. It makes one dependent on one's own means of forces, makes one feel lonely and frightened. The use of force is a possible answer to life, but it is an absurd one, not only because of the shaky quality of force, but mainly because in the most crucial phenomenon of existence, the inevitability of death, force will not help. The most powerful man is defeated by death, just as is the most powerless one, and it is this sting of ultimate defeat that makes the principle of force so ludicrous, even though not necessarily on a conscious level.

Love is always an active concern for the growth and aliveness of the one we love. It cannot be otherwise; since life itself is a process of becoming, of unification and integration, love for all that is alive must be the passionate desire to further this growth. On the other hand, as we have seen, the wish to control and the wish to use force are contrary to the nature of love, and are an obstacle to its development and functioning.

But, some of you will impatiently ask now, why talk about the love of life, when you have so far mainly talked about the love for persons or animals or plants? Is there such a thing as "love for life"? Is it not perhaps an abstraction, and the only real objects of love are specific and concrete phenomena like people?

I believe I have already answered part of this question, or at least I have laid the foundation for an answer. If the nature of life is that of being a process of growth and integration, if it cannot be loved by means of control or force, love for life is the kernel of all love; it is the love for the life in a person, in an animal, in a flower. Love for life, far from being an abstraction is the most concrete nucleus in any kind of love. Anyone who believes he loves a person and who does not love also life, may desire, want, cling to a person—but he does not love him.

That this is so is known to us, although we are often not consciously aware of this knowledge. When someone says about a person that "he really loves life," most people understand precisely what is meant. We refer to a person who loves all phenomena of growth and aliveness, one who is attracted to a growing child, the growth in an adult, a growing idea, a growing organization. To him, even that which is not alive, like a stone or water, becomes alive and that which is alive attracts him not because it is big and powerful, but because it is alive. Often you can even recognize the lover of life by his facial expression. There is a radiance in his eye and also in his skin, something glowing in and around him. When people "fall in love," they love life, and that is the reason they attract each other. But if this love of life is too weak to last, they fall out of love again and do not understand why their faces are the same and yet not the same any longer.

Is the love of life something in which people differ only in degree? How good if this were so, but, unfortunately, there are people who do not love life, who "love" death, destruction, illness, decay, disintegration. They are not attracted by growth and aliveness, except that they dislike and want to strangle them. They hate life because they cannot enjoy it or control it. They suffer from the only true perversion that exists—i.e., to be attracted to death. In my book *The Heart of Man* (1964a), I have called these people necrophiles, "lovers of death," and indicated that the necrophilous orientation, in its extreme forms, is, from a psychiatric point of view, indicative of severe mental illness.

If you observe and watch, you will discover that you have known lovers of death as well as lovers of life; but perhaps you did not dare to think in these terms, because on the surface everyone is "nice" and "loving," and when it happens that a man is gripped by the desire to kill people, we tend to shrug off his condition by calling him "sick." He may be sick, but how can we be sure that we, too, do not suffer from this same sickness? What makes us so certain we are lovers of life rather than lovers of death?

Actually, there are grave symptoms in our culture today that suggest we are already infected by an insidious attraction to that which is not alive. We see manifestations of this attraction all around us: destructive violence and sadism on the inter-

205

national level, crime and cruelty on the national level; the degree of tension and anxiety, which can almost be measured quantitatively by the amount of tranquilizing pills sold in our country; drug addiction, which is an effort to substitute thrills and excitement for a genuine love of life. We do not need statistics to be convinced. Most of us show the symptoms in one degree or another. Consider the need so many of us have to take a drink before we can be comfortable in company; our synthetic expressions of gaiety and sorrow when the occasion seems to demand them; our tendency to think rather than to feel what is appropriate to the situation (a wedding, a funeral, the painting of a celebrated artist); the increasing use of sex to achieve "intimacy" and excitement without any feeling toward the other person except desire.

Another evidence for anxiety and tension is compulsive cigarette smoking. Anyone who has tried to stop smoking has made the experience that the temptation is greatest when he is to meet people, or in any other situation which makes him afraid or tense.

You can make another observation. Try to sit still, to do nothing, and to think nothing. Maybe you shut your eyes, maybe you look at a tree, a field, a flower. You may think that this is simple. Try it! You may find yourself getting restless, thinking about a hundred and one things, just waiting for the moment when you can end the experiment.

Is all this tension and anxiety your personal problem? To some extent, of course, these symptoms are individual problems; but to a larger extent they are the result of our way of living in the industrial age. First of all, we are more concerned with results than with the process that leads to them. These results, in the sphere of industrial production, are brought about by machines and gadgets, and it has reached a point where we consider ourselves as machines, too, expect quick results, and look for gadgets that produce the desired effect.

But we are not machines! Life is not a means to an end; it is an end in itself; the process of living, that is, of changing, growing, developing, being more aware and more awake, is more important than any mechanical achievement or result— if, and this is a very important qualification—we love life. If you were asked why you love another person and answered, "because he is successful, famous, rich," you would probably feel a little uneasy, because you know all this has nothing to do with love. But if you would say, because he or she is very alive, that you love his or her smile, voice, hands, eyes be- cause they radiate life, then, indeed, you would have given a reason. It is not different with yourself. You are interesting because you are interested. You are loved because you can love and because in yourself and in the other person you love life.

This attitude, however, is difficult to experience in a culture that emphasizes results instead of processes, things instead of life, that makes means into ends and that teaches us to use the brain when the heart should be involved. Love for another person and love for life are not something that can be achieved in a hurry. Sex, yes, but not love. Love requires pleasure in stillness, an ability to enjoy *being* instead of *doing, having,* or *using.*

Another factor that makes it difficult to love life is our in- creasing, never satisfied appetite for things. True enough, things can, and should, serve man; but if they become ends rather than remain means, they tend to sap man's interest in and love for life and to make him an appendix of the machine, a thing. Things can produce many results, but they cannot love, either a person or life. We have been so indoctrinated as consumers that we have come to believe that almost no plea- sure is complete unless it includes something you can buy. We have lost the knowledge that a few generations ago was quite widespread: that the most exquisite pleasures of life do not require gadgets. But they do require the capacity for stillness, for "letting go," for concentration.

Travel to the moon, which excites the fantasy of millions of people, is more fascinating to most than giving oneself fully to looking at a person, a flower, a river, or into oneself. Certainly, in the travel-to-the-moon orientation there are intelligence, perseverance, courage, daring, but there is no love. Travel to the moon is only a symbol of living with mechanical gadgets, admiring them and using them. This world of man-made things and their use is our pride and our danger. The more the "thing" aspect of the world becomes prominent, the more we are interested in the manipulation of these things, the less we experience the quality of life, and the less can we love life. Indeed, there is reason to suspect that we are more fond of the technical miracles that can destroy life than we are of life itself. Could it be that the people of the industrialized world do not succeed in achieving effective nuclear disarmament because life has lost much of its attraction and things have become the object of our admiration?

Still another obstacle to loving life is the ever increasing bureaucratization of our activities. You can choose nicer names for it: "teamwork," "group spirit," or whatever you like. The essential fact, however, is that, for the sake of maximal economic efficiency, we tend to cut each individual down to the proper size that makes it possible for him to become one of the group; efficient, disciplined, but not himself, not fully alive and hence paralyzed in his capacity to love life.

But what can we do to change all this, you may well ask at this point. Is it necessary to give up our system of mass production, our technical achievements, in order to love life again? I do not think so. But what is necessary is to be aware of the danger, to put material things in their place, to cease transforming ourselves into things and manipulators of things. If instead of manipulating, we love all that is alive, then even a thing, a glass, for instance, can become alive through our life-giving approach to it, such as the artist has. Then we shall learn that if you look at someone or something long enough, he or it will talk to you. But you must truly look, forget about getting something out of it and be able to be really still. If you find it necessary to describe your feelings with enraptured statements like "Isn't it divine" or "I am dying to see it again," then your sentiments are not likely to be worth much; if you can look at a tree in such a way that it seems to be looking back at you, you probably will not feel like saying anything.

There are no prescriptions for loving life, but much can be learned. If you can shed illusions, seeing others and yourself as they are and you are, if you can learn how to be still rather than always "going places," if you can grasp the distinction between life and things, between happiness and thrill, between means and ends, and—most of all—between love and force, you will have made the first steps toward loving life. After you have made these first steps, ask again. You will find meaningful answers in a number of books—and most of all within yourself.

One question should not be ignored: You might be afraid that the more one loves life the more one suffers from the hourly assault on truth, beauty, integrity, and life. Indeed this is so and especially today. But to save oneself from pain by becoming indifferent to life produces only greater pain. Any severely depressed person can tell you that to feel sad would be a relief from the torture of feeling nothing. Happiness is not the most important thing in life—aliveness is. Suffering is not the worst thing in life—indifference is.

One more remark: If we suffer, we might try to stop the causes of suffering. If we feel nothing, we are paralyzed. Thus far in human history, suffering has been the midwife of change. Should, for the first time, indifference destroy man's capacity to change his fate?

# Bibliography

Ayres, C. E. 1927. "Review of Robert Briffault, The Mothers." *The New Republic* (12 April 1927).

Bachofen, J. J. 1926. *Das Mutterrecht*. In *Der Mythos von Orient und Occident: Eine Metaphysik der alten Welt*, edited by Manfred Schroeter. With an introduction by Alfred Bäumler. Munich: C. H. Beck'sche Verlagsbuchhandlung.

————. 1954. *Mutterrecht und Urreligion, eine Auswahl, herausgegeben von Rudolf Marx*. Kröners Taschenausgabe, vol. 52. Stuttgart: Alfred Kröner Verlag.

————. 1967. *Myth, Religion, and Mother Right*. In *Selected Writings of J. J. Bachofen* [see J. J. Bachofen 1954]. Translated from the German by Ralph Manheim, with a Preface by George Boas and an Introduction by Joseph Cambell. Bollingen Series, no. 84. Princeton: Princeton University Press.

Bäumler, A. 1926. "Bachofen, der Mythologe der Romantik." In *Der Mythos von Orient und Occident: Eine Metaphysik der alten Welt*. With an introduction by Alfred Bäumler. Munich: C. H. Beck'sche Verlagsbuchhandlung. New edition entitled *Das Mythische Weltalter. Bachofens ro-*

*mantische Deutung des Altertums.* With an Afterword, "Bachofen und die Religionsgeschichte." Munich: Verlag C. H. Beck, 1965.

Bebel, A. 1878. *Die Frau und der Sozialismus.* Stuttgart: Dietz Nachf.

Bender, L., and Schilder, P. 1936. "Aggressiveness in Children." *Genetic Psychology Monographs* 18 (1936): 410–25.

Briffault, R. 1928. *The Mothers: A Study of the Origins of Sentiment and Institutions.* 3 vols. London: G. Allen and Unwin, Ltd.

Calvin, J. 1955. *Institutes of the Christian Religion.* Translated by John Allen. Philadelphia: Presbyterian Board of Christian Education.

Darwin, Ch. R. 1858. *On the Origin of Species by Means of Natural Selection.* London: J. Murray.

Despert, J. L. 1940. "A Method for the Study of Personality Reactions in Preschool Age Children by Means of Analysis of Their Play." *Journal of Psychology* 9 (1940): 17–29.

Ellis, H. 1928. "Review of Robert Briffault, *The Mothers.*" *Birth Control Review* (September); and in *Views and Reviews,* 2nd Series: 160f.

Engels, F. 1962. *Der Ursprung der Familie, des Privateigentums und des Staats.* In Karl Marx and Friedrich Engels, *Werke* (MEW), vol. 21. Berlin: Dietz Verlag, pp. 25–173 and 473–83.

Fourier, Ch. 1878. *Die Frau und der Sozialismus.*

Freud, S. 1953–1974. *The Standard Edition of the Complete Psychological Works of Sigmund Freud* (S. E.). 24 vols. London: The Hogarth Press.

———. 1900a. *The Interpretation of Dreams.* S. E., vols. 4 and 5.

———. 1924d. *The Dissolution of the Oedipus Complex.* S. E., vol. 19, pp. 171–79.

———. 1930a. *Civilization and Its Discontent.* S. E., vol. 21, pp. 57–145.

———. 1953. *Civilization and Its Discontent.* Translated by J. Riviere. London: The Hogarth Press Ltd.

Fromm, E. 1932a. "The Method and Function of an Analytic Social Psychology." In *The Crisis of Psychoanalysis.* New York: Holt, Rinehart and Winston, 1970, pp. 135–62.

———. 1932b. "Psychoanalytic Characterology and Its Relevance for Social Psychology." In *The Crisis of Psychoanalysis.* New York: Holt, Rinehart and Winston, 1970, pp. 163–89.

———. 1933a. "Robert Briffaults Werk über das Mutterrecht." In *Zeitschrift für Sozialforschung.* Paris: Librairie Félix Alcan, vol. 2, pp. 382–87.

———. 1934a. "The Theory of Mother Right and Its Relevance for Social Psychology." In *The Crisis of Psychoanalysis.* New York: Holt, Rinehart and Winston, 1970, pp. 106–34.

———. 1936a. "Sozialpsychologischer Teil." In *Schriften des Instituts für Sozialforschung,* vol. V: Studien über Autorität und Familie. Forschungsberichte aus dem Institut für Sozialforschung, Paris 1936, pp. 77–135 (Félix Alcan).

———. 1941a. *Escape from Freedom.* New York: Farrar and Rinehart.

———. 1943b. "Sex and Character." *Psychiatry: Journal for the Study of Interpersonal Process* 6 (1943): pp. 21–31.

———. 1947a. *Man for Himself.* New York: Rinehart and Co.

————. 1949b. "The Oedipus Complex and the Oedipus Myth." In *The Family: Its Functions and Destiny*. Edited by R. N. Anshen. New York: Harper & Bros, pp. 334–58.

————. 1951a. *The Forgotten Language*. New York: Rinehart and Co.

————. 1951b. "Man–Woman." In *The People in Your Life: Psychiatry and Personal Relations*. Edited by M. M. Hughes. New York: Alfred A. Knopf. pp. 3–27.

————. 1964a. *The Heart of Man: Its Genius for Good and Evil*. New York: Harper and Row.

Fromm-Reichmann, F. 1940. "Notes on the Mother Role in the Family Group." *Bulletin of the Menninger Clinic* 4 (1940): 132–48.

Ginsberg, M. 1927. "Review of Robert Briffault, The Mothers." *The Nation and the Antheneum* (20 August 1928).

Goldenweiser, A. 1928. "Review of Robert Briffault, The Mothers." *The Nation* (20 July 1928).

Horkheimer, M. 1936. "Egoismus und Freiheitsbewegung." *Zeitschrift für Sozialforschung* 5 (1936).

Horney, K. 1932. "Die Angst vor der Frau." *Internationale Zeitschrift für Psychoanalyse* 13 (1932): 1–18.

————. 1937. *The Neurotic Personality of Our Time*. New York: W. W. Norton & Co.

————. 1939. *New Ways in Psychoanalysis*. New York: W. W. Norton & Co.

James, W. 1893. *Principles of Psychology*. 2 vols. New York: Holt.

Jones, E. 1953. *The Life and Work of Sigmund Freud*, vol. 1. New York: Basic Books, Inc.

Kant, I. 1907. *Die Religion innerhalb der Grenzen der bloßen Vernunft.* In *Immanuel Kants Werke*, vol. 6. Berlin: Georg Reimer Verlag; engl.: *Religion Within the Limits of Reason Alone*. Translated by Th. M. Greene and H. H. Hudson. Chicago: Open Court, 1934.

———. 1907a. *Der Rechtslehre Zweiter Teil: Das öffentliche Recht.* In *Immanuel Kants Werke*, vol. 6. Berlin: Georg Reimer Verlag.

———. 1908. *Kritik der praktischen Vernunft.* In *Immanuel Kants Werke*, vol. 5. Berlin: Georg Reimer Verlag; engl.: *Kant's Critique of Practical Reason and Other Works on the Theory of Ethics*. Translated by Thomas Kingsmill Abbot. London, New York: Longmans Greene, 1909.

Kelles-Krauz, C. von. 1975. "J. J. Bachofen." In *Materialien zu Bachofens "Das Mutterrecht."* Edited by Hans-Jürgen Heinnchs. Frankfurt: Suhrkamp Verlag, pp. 75–86; reprint of "J. J. Bachofen (1861–1901): Aus den Studien über die Quellen des Marxismus." Lecture published in *Die Neue Zeit*. Revue des geistigen und öffentlichen Lebens, Stuttgart Nr. 15, XX. Jahrgang, I. Band 1901–1902, pp. 517–24.

Kluckhohn, P. 1931. *Die Auffassung der Liebe in der Literatur des 18. Jahrhunderts und in der Romantik.* Halle: Niemeyer.

Kraus, J. B. 1930. *Scholastik, Puritanismus und Kapitalismus.* Munich: Dunker.

Langdon-Davies, J. 1927. "Review of Robert Briffault, The Mothers." *The Herald Tribune* (18 September 1927).

Levy, D. M. 1937. *Studies in Sibling Rivalry*, vol. 5. New York: American Orthopsychiatric Association.

Ludovici, A. M. 1927. "Review of Robert Briffault, The Mothers." *English Review* (November).

Lynd, R. S. 1939. *Knowledge for What*. Princeton: Princeton University Press.

Malinowski, B. 1927. "Review of Robert Briffault, The Mothers." *Statesman* (September).

Marx, K. *Karl Marx und Friedrich Engels, Historisch-kritische Gesamtausgabe. Werke—Schriften—Briefe, im Auftrag des Marx-Engels-Lenin-Instituts Moskau*. Edited by V. Adoratskij. Sämtliche Werke und Schriften mit Ausnahme des Kapital, vol. 1. Berlin, 1932.

Marx, K., and Engels, F. *Werke* (MEW). Berlin: Dietz Verlag.

———. 1961. *Zur Kritik der Politischen Ökonomie*. In MEW, vol. 13, pp. 3–160.

———. 1962. *Der Ursprung der Familie, des Privateigentums und des Staats*. With reference to Lewis H. Morgan's research, with the introduction to the 4th edition of 1891. In MEW, vol. 21, pp. 25–173 and 473–83.

Morgan, L. H. 1870. *Systems of Sanguinity and Affinity of the Human Family*. Publication 218. Washington: Smithsonian Inst.

———. 1877. *Ancient Society: Or Researches in the Lines of Human Progress from Savagery Through Barbarism to Civilization*. New York: H. Holt.

Nietzsche, F. 1906. *Götzen-Dämmerung*. In *Nietzsches Werke*, Sect. I, vol. 8. Leipzig: A. Kröner Verlag; engl.: *The Twilight of Idols*. Translated by A. M. Ludovici. Edinburgh: T. N. Foulis, 1911.

———. 1910. *Also sprach Zarathustra*. In *Nietzsches Werke*, Sect. I. vol. 6. Leipzig: A. Kröner Verlag; engl.: *Thus Spake Zarathustra*. Translated by Thomas Common. New York: Modern Library.

———. 1910a. *Zur Genealogie der Moral*. In *Nietzsches Werke*, Sect. I, vol. 7. Leipzig: A. Kröner Verlag; engl.: *Beyond Good and Evil*. Translated by Helen Zimmer. New York: Macmillan, 1907.

———. 1911. *Der Wille zur Macht*. In *Nietzsches Werke*. Sect. II, vol. 15 and 16. Leipzig: A. Kröner Verlag; engl.: *The Will to Power*. Translated by Anthony M. Ludovici. 2 vols. Edinburgh and London: T. N. Foulis, 1910.

———. 1911a. *Ecce Homo*. In *Nietzsches Werke*. Sect. II, vol. 15. Leipzig: A. Kröner Verlag; engl.: *Ecce Homo*. Translated by A. M. Ludovici. New York: Macmillan, 1911.

———. *Nachlaß: Nietzsches Werke*. Leipzig: A. Kroener Verlag.

Pascal, R. 1933. *The Social Basis of the German Reformation: Martin Luther and His Times*. London: Watts.

Reich, W. 1933. *Charakteranalyse. Technik und Grundlagen*. Vienna: Verlag für Sexualpolitik.

Robeson (Brown), A. 1927. *The Portrait of a Banker: James Stillmann*. New York: Duffield.

Spinoza, Baruch de. 1976. *Die Ethik*. Hamburg: Felix Meiner Verlag.

Stirner, M. 1893. *Der Einzige und sein Eigentum*. Leipzig: Philipp Reclam jun.; engl.: *The Ego and His Own*. Translated by Steven T. Byington. London: A. C. Fifield, 1912.

Sullivan, H. S. 1940. "Conceptions of Modern Psychiatry: The First William Alanson White Memorial Lectures." *Psychiatry* 3 (1940), 1–117.

Tawney, R. H. 1926. *Religion and the Rise of Capitalism.* London: John Murray.

Thompson, C. 1942. "What Is Penis Envy?" In *Proceedings of the Association for the Advancement of Psychoanalysis,* Boston Meetings 1942.

Ungnad, A. 1921. *Die Religion der Babylonier und Assyrer.* Religiöse Stimmen der Völker, Walter Otto, vol. 3. Jena: Eugen Diederichs Verlag.

Weber, M. 1920. *Die protestantische Ethik und der Geist des Kapitalismus.* In *Gesammelte Aufsätze zur Religionssoziologie,* vol. 1. Tübingen: J. C. B. Mohr; engl.: *The Protestant Ethic and the Spirit of Capitalism.* Translated by Talcott Parsons. London: Allan, 1930.

Weininger, O. 1903. *Geschlecht und Charakter.* Vienna.

# Sources and Copyrights

1. "Bachofen's Discovery of the Mother Right," 1955 (?), posthumous papers, New York City Public Library. © 1994 by the estate of Erich Fromm.

2. "The Theory of Mother Right and Its Relevance for Social Psychology," *The Crisis of Psychoanalysis: Essays on Freud, Marx, and Social Psychology* (New York: Holt Rinehart Winston, 1970), pp. 84–109.

3. "Die männliche Schöfung," 1933 (?), posthumous papers, New York City Public Library. © 1994 by the estate of Erich Fromm.

4. "Robert Briffaults Werk über das Mutterrecht," *Zeitschrift für Sozialforschung* (Paris: Librairie Félix Alcan), II (1933), 382–387. Reprinted in Erich Fromm, *Gesamtausgabe in 10 Bänden* (Stuttgart 1980 and Munich 1989), I, 79–84.

5. "The Significance of the Theory of Mother Right for Today," in Erich Fromm, *The Crisis of Psychoanalysis: Essays on Freud, Marx and Social Psychology* (New York: Holt Rinehart Winston, 1970), pp. 79–83.

6. "Sex and Character," *Psychiatry: Journal for the Study of Interpersonal Process* (Washington: The William Alanson Psychiatric Foundation) 6 (1943): 21–31. An expanded version appeared in R. N. Anshen, ed., *The*

*Family: Its Functions and Destiny* (New York: Harper and Row, 1949), pp. 375–92.

7. "Man–Woman," Prepared under the auspices of Town Hall, New York, ed. Margaret M. Hughes, with a foreword by Isabel Leighton, *The People of Your Life: Psychiatry and Personal Relations by Ten Leading Authorities* (New York: Alfred A. Knopf, 1951), pp. 3–27.

8. "Sex and Character: The Kinsey Report Viewed from the Standpoint of Psychoanalysis," ed. D. P. Geddes and E. Curie, *About the Kinsey Report* (New York: The New American Library, 1948), pp. 301–11.

9. "Changing Concepts of Homosexuality," 1940 (?), posthumous papers, New York City Public Library; © 1994 by the estate of Erich Fromm.

10. "Selfishness and Self-Love," *Psychiatry: Journal for the Study of Interpersonal Process* (Washington: The William Alanson Psychiatric Foundation) 2 (1939): 507–23.

11. "Do We Still Love Life?" *McCall's* (Los Angeles: McCall Publishing Co), vol. 94 (August 1967): 57 and 108–110.